A mind's piece

A mind's piece : Poetry collection

Published by Chaplins Publishing
Pasadena, California, 91107
chaplinspublishing.com

Library of Congress Control Number: 2026907396
ISBN: 979-8-9953618-0-0 (Paperback)
ISBN: 979-8-9953618-1-7 (eBook)

Printed in the United States of America.

A mind's piece

Poetry collection

Sue Chaplin

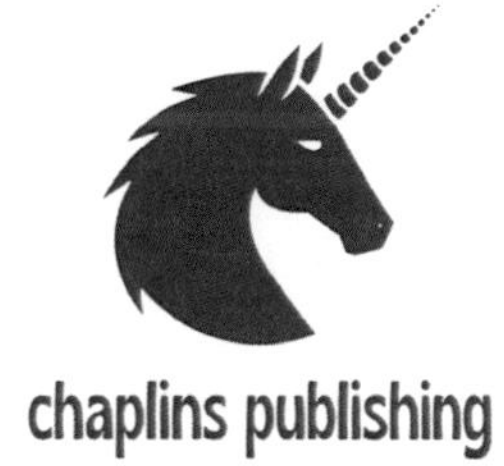

Dedication

My sons, Peter & Gavin, the lights of my life, I love you always,

My love, Alain, you have shown me the beauty of true love and believed in my poetry,

My amazing parents, Jan & Gary, you are always there for me, you are my inspiration,

My sister, Karen, the best sister in the world, who rides with me even when it's crazy,

My best friend, Lia, traveling life's road with the amazing you has meant everything to me,

All of you, thank you for sharing your time with me.

May love be with you always.

"Always be yourself,
unless you can be a unicorn.

Then, be a unicorn."

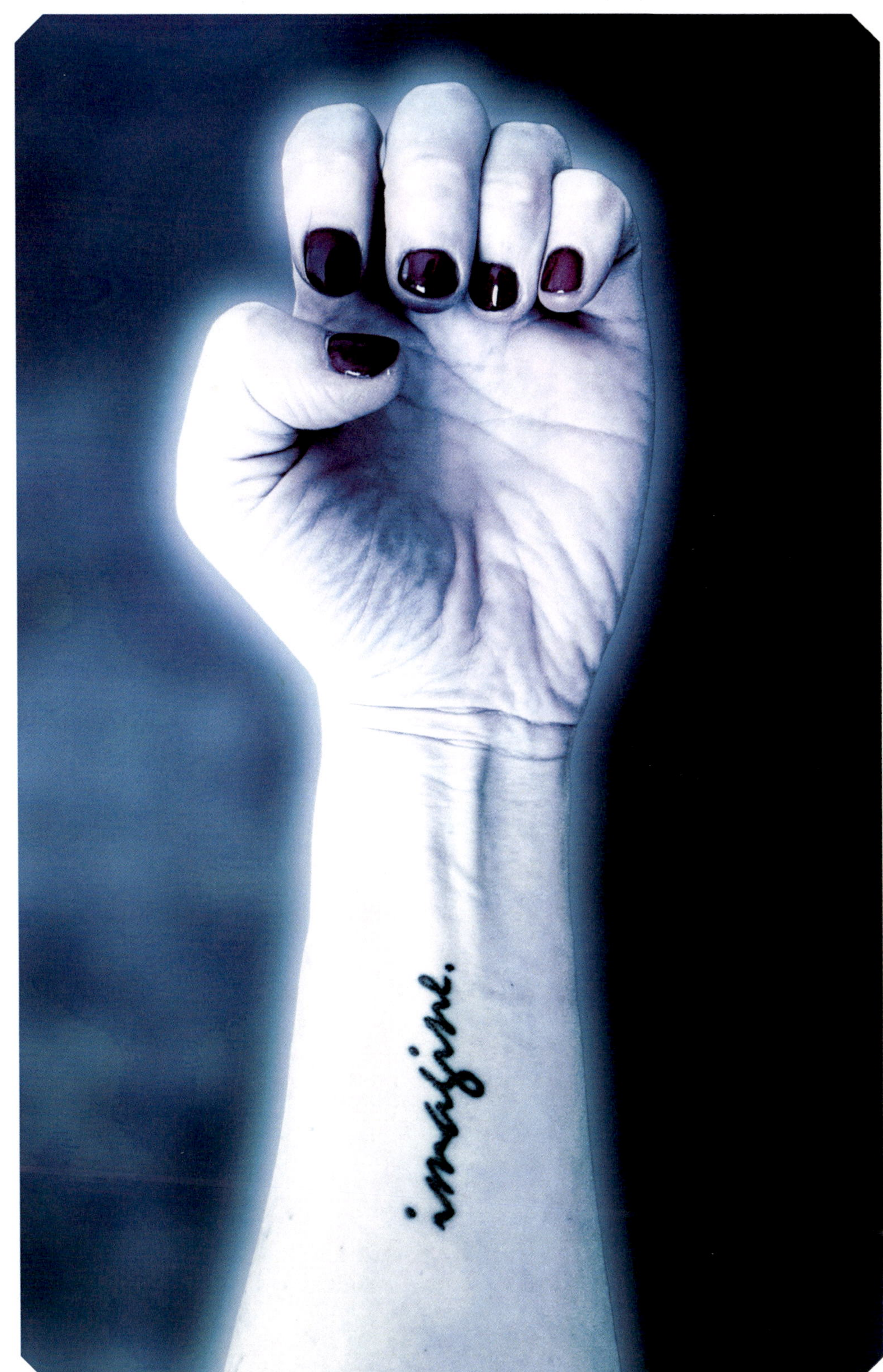
imagine.

Contents

PREFACE

In love and life, we rise and fall. I began this poetry journey in the spring of 2020, during the pandemic in my Pasadena, California home. I wrote poetry as a child, and the intense feelings that overcame me during this trying time, revealed my love again. I experienced the beauty of creating art of life's good and bad moments. I could quietly retreat and capture footprints in my life's journey.

Throughout this time, I experienced so many struggles and fantasies, hand in hand: the pandemic, the loss and recovery of my hearing, the loss of my marriage, the trials of life-threatening illness, and the Altadena fires, but also the heavens of new love, the passion for work, and the precious moments spent with my two amazing sons, Peter and Gavin, who were growing up before my eyes. It was a time of overcoming hardship, experiencing great joy and exploring my imagination in between. These poems became my little world and my place of dreams. I never thought they'd be more than my private sanctuary of treasures.

Along the way, what began as a photo app I used to retouch my headshot, became experimentation with my iPhone library, exploring a visual portrayal of life moments. With layers of filters and AI tools on these photographs, I could construct a bridge between reality and fantasy in my poetry, bringing it to life in a new way. With the intent of exploring the imagination's dimensions in everyday life, I have presented my photos as art with my written works.

These poems appear in the order they were written, as a journey through this intense and unprecedented time in my life. They include "Total darkness," refreshed from the version published in my high school literary magazine. In the heartfelt spirit of the poem, "The end of the beginning," I realized this chapter in my life had ended. I wanted to share these poems with you so they may be a glimmer of light in both dark and joyous times.

I could describe what the poems are about to me, but I hope it is more about what they are for you when you read them. To catalog my heartache and elation during these years, questioning whether I had my fair share of each, I know I have only lived the joys and the pains of the human experience we all traverse, captured through my eyes and heart. For those who supported me on this journey, I would not be writing these words without you. You are the air that I breathe. Thank you for all your love, now and forever.

Sue Chaplin

A mind’s piece

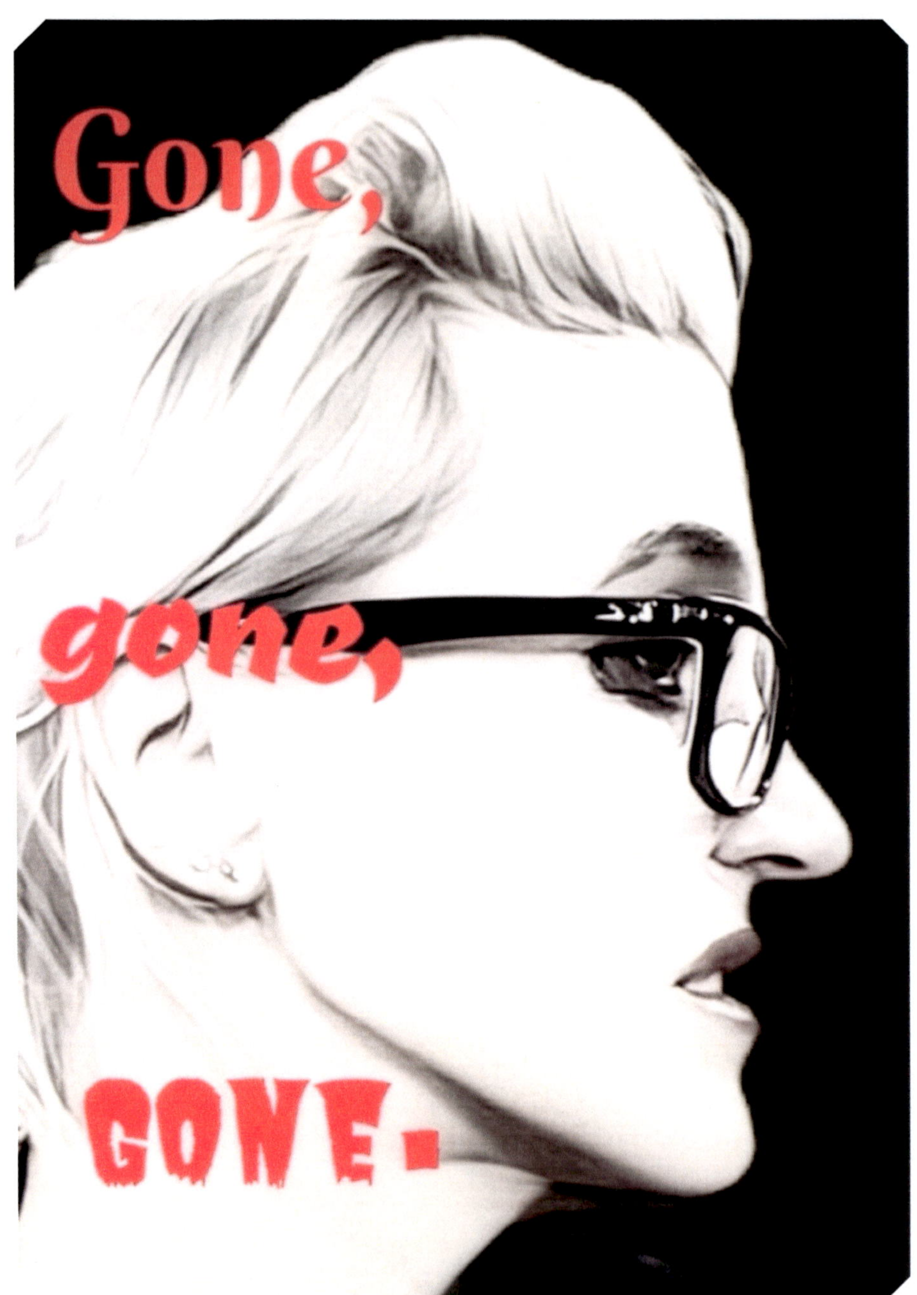
Gone,
gone,
GONE.

Gone, gone, gone.
The time you knew would come is here.
Moments fleeting with clenched hands,
Finally slipped through fingers,
Sand.
The signs were there, so hard to face.
It dissipates then leaves no trace.
Claw back memories to no use.
Feelings felt, compelled – not true.
You knew this time would come,
It's here.
Life is what it is,
Is true.

The darkness in my heart.
Your constance is a comfort, my friend.
You are my anchor to the ground.
Yet compel me, thrust me without fear.
The depth so low turns to abandon.
Without a floor, I explore no limits.
Flower grows, roots deep in soil.
All see the bloom, not what's beneath.
Dark richness fuels the color and shape.
Of what is loved, and then unknown.
Moments misunderstood,
Darkness exposed.
Feelings that planted the seed inside.
The beauty is true, as is the mark,
Of what, too, is alive.

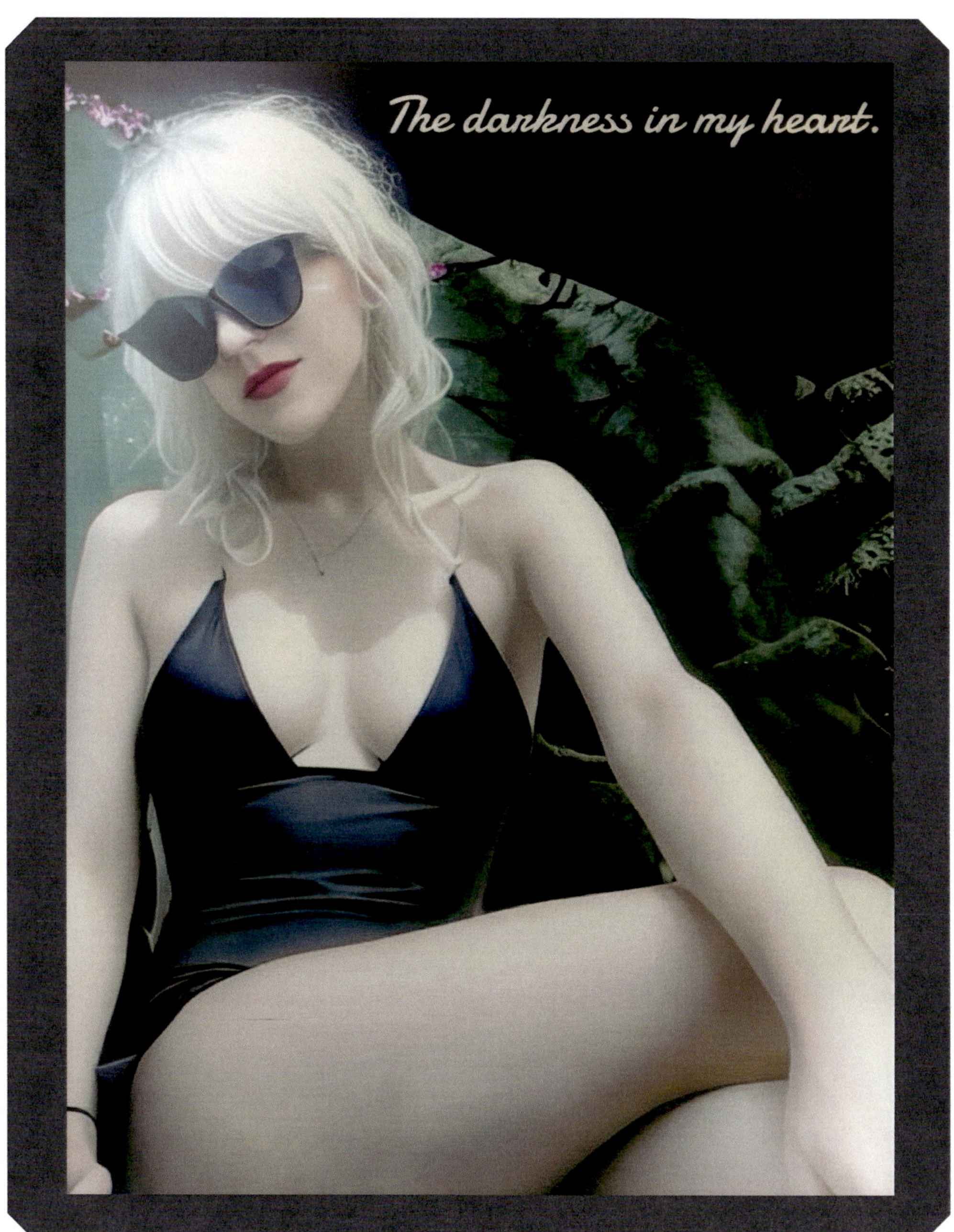
The darkness in my heart.

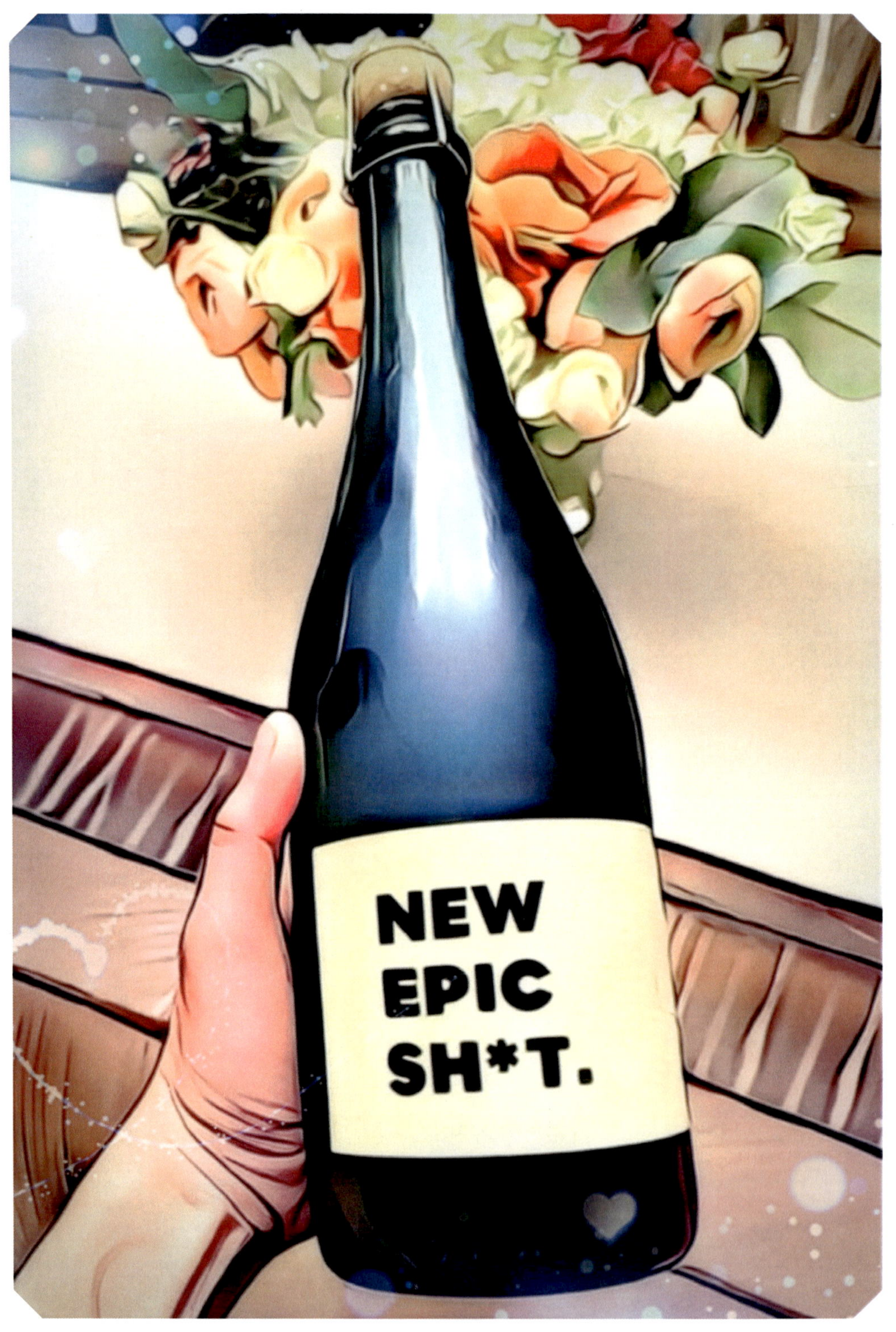
NEW
EPIC
SH*T.

Letting go.

At dusk, the light of day
Dims to fade.
The stir of the breeze, picks up, takes hold.
Sitting still, alone, we breathe as one -
The trees rustle, the air flows, and me.
The day is letting go, and then I know,
So can I.
I open my closed hands, and feel the wind lift it away.
What I need to let go.
With eyes damp, my heart aches,
I hope that I can heal.
Thoughts that imaginations can be real,
Cannot be held but freed.
They are the fuel but cannot be.
Not to be touched,
Closeness too much.
I feel the breeze lift them away.
And once again I am alone.
Just me,
And I am still.

Do we all want?
Or is it mine to crave,
Just crawling in my mind.
In a room I sit,
Others talk, I'm there.
Just me that feels there's more.
The scales tilt from me.
I watch, apart.
It's what I have, yet I'm without.
Do we all want?
But unknown, can't reach.
Or where it lies, it's not our path.
If we faced it, fears' too much?
Comfort's now just tastes too rich.
Don't touch the ache,
Push it down.
Pacify.
Words fill empty rooms.
The haunting need hums too soft,
Exposed to some, yet not enough.
The tug and push yield no swing,
Balanced on weightless depth.
Time will tell, but not for now.
Trapped in silence, I'm without.

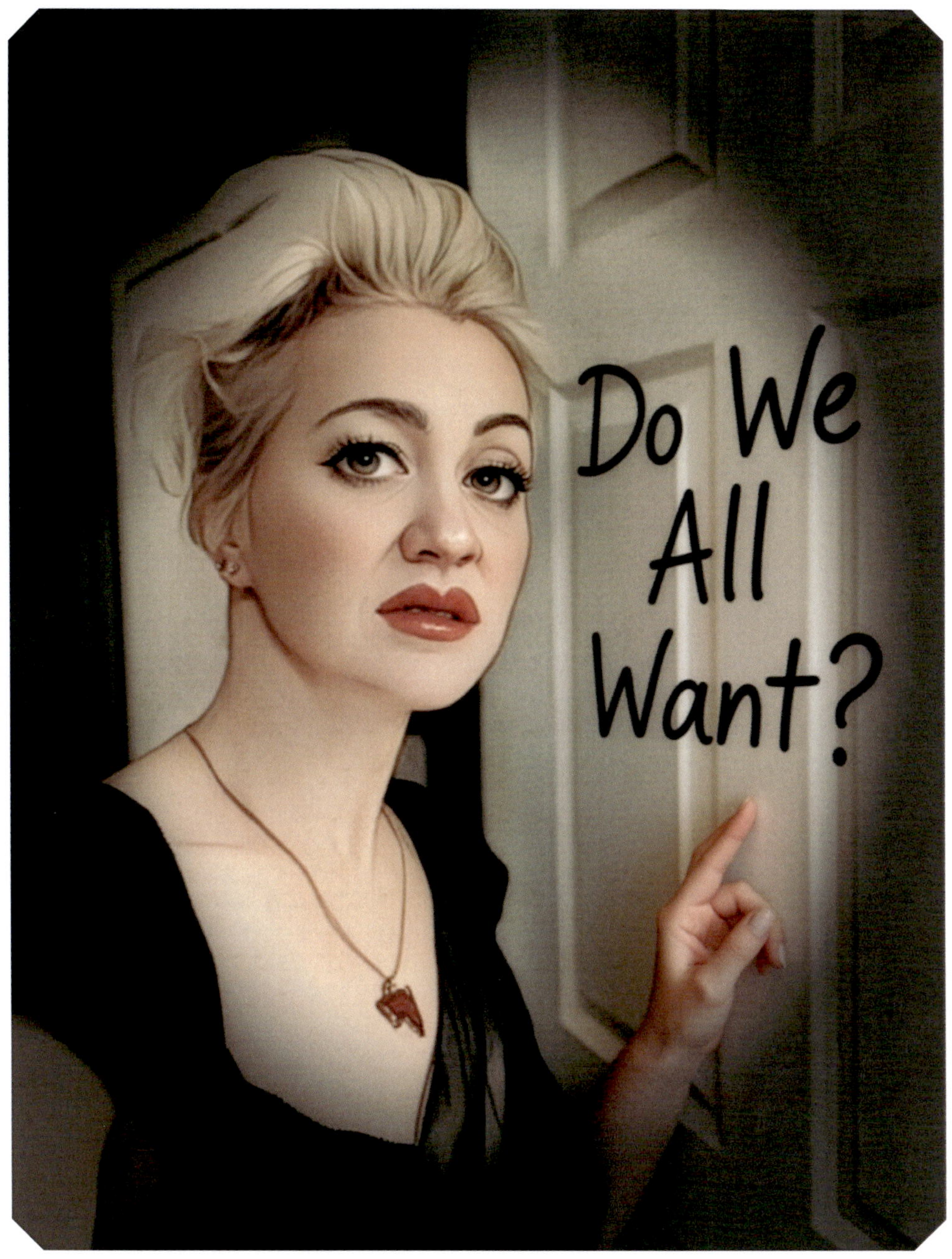
Do We
All
Want?

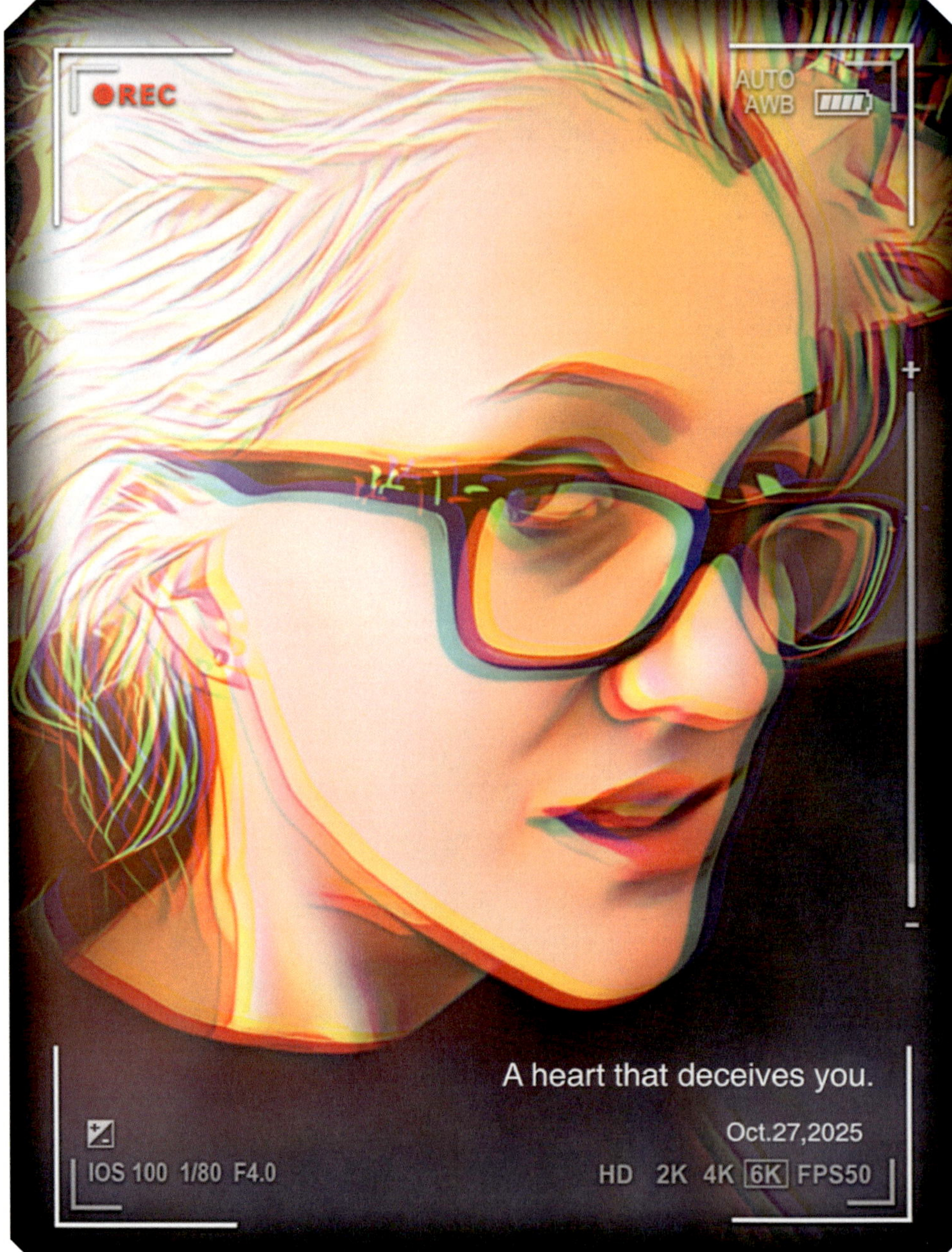
REC
AUTO
AWB
A heart that deceives you.
Oct.27,2025
IOS 100 1/80 F4.0
HD 2K 4K 6K FPS50

A heart that deceives you.
A mind that gives way.
It swells and enrapts you
Over moments of day.
You go where it takes you,
Overtakes, don't resist.
You wouldn't now loving
The feelings' deep kiss.
Moments on surface
You're a lifetime away.
Awash in your image,
Can't touch then it fades.
You savor the times of your alternate ways,
And it's there you can live it, though secret it stays.
You let it addict you, the feelings divine.
When you steal moments, you seek till you find.
But it is a deception that pulls you away.
They see that you're elsewhere and then you can't stay.
You say that you'll stop it, life's real, it's not fake.
But your heart it deceives you, and that path you take.

You find your peace.
The world it wears on you and bends,
It thrusts you to the ground.
On hands and knees, you gather breath,
Not knowing where you're found.
Nothing feels the same
You thought you knew this place you live.
Every day you're here
You felt and touched,
But that was real does not exist.
What does it mean to live at all?
When all you had is gone?

Yet in a quiet still of breath,
Your heart beats,
You feel the drum.

With all around you every day,
Somehow it fades, obscured.
But it's always there, its truth is real,
Heartfelt and it's yours.
You find your peace, never lost could be,
Life is the purest gift.
The illusion was, not ever gone.
Yours today,
Deep within kept all along.

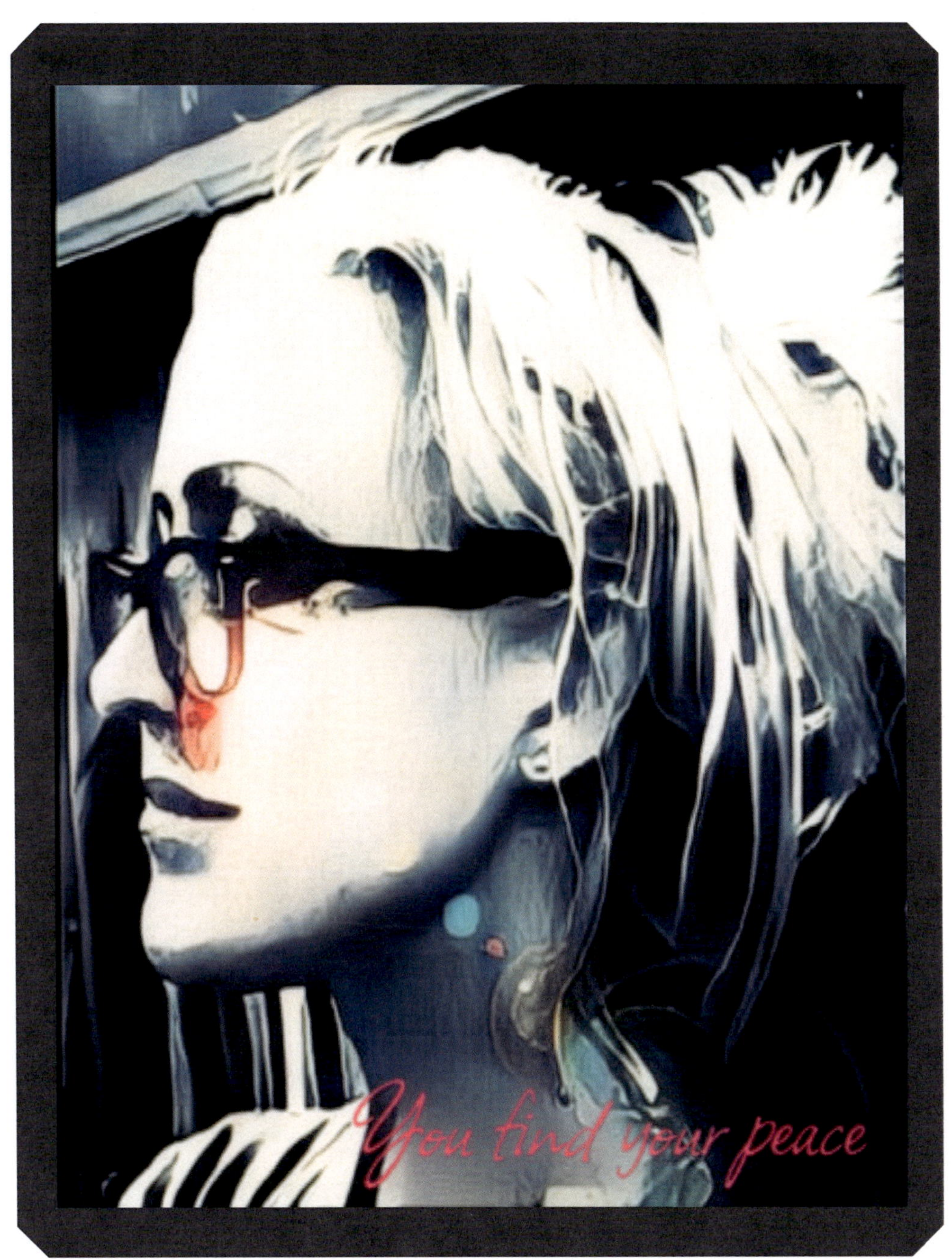
You find your peace

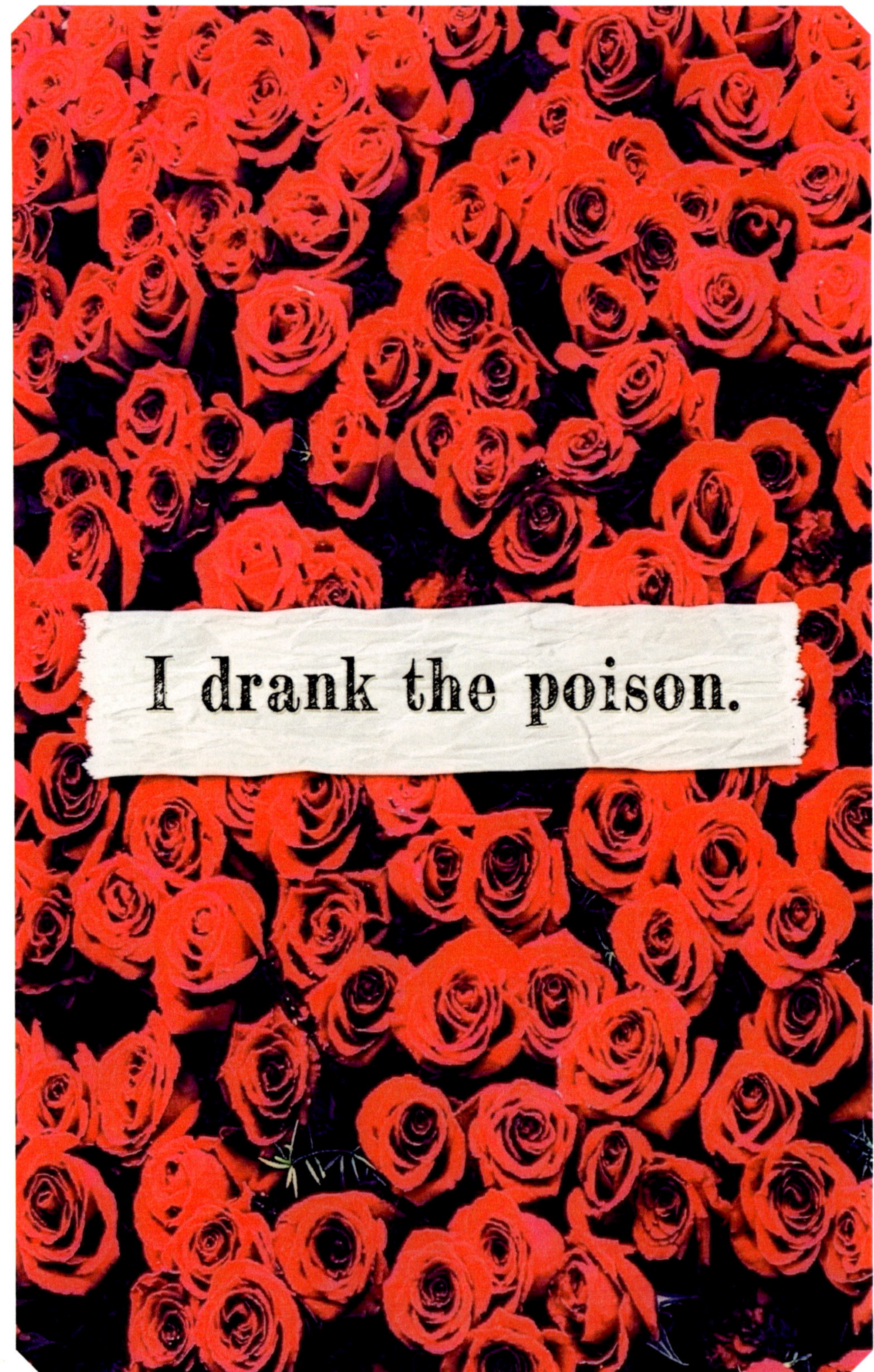
I drank the poison.

I drank the poison.
There it sat, the poison.
Framed in dark instinct, it holds me.
In a moment of impulse, I reached and swallowed it down,
A rush so irresistible.
A sweet burn slips past my taste, veiled, revealing none.
Ice races through my veins, needles pierce my skin.
The swell of my pounding heart, drumming so hard, drowns my senses.
My first pass of expectation, unknowing what could be different.
Yet compulsion's thrill is not what I seek.
Waiting, I feel nothing.
Once electric, now an unsteady calm.
Stagnating air, the room resets.
Light returns to life's pace,
It was nothing.
I begin to gather my steps.

Then it hits me.

Like a thousand throws of the most powerful force.
Like nothing before, seducing and incredible, I feel it overtake me pleasure and pain.
I'm carried with the rushing current. An undertow that surrounds me from everywhere.
I try to regain what I so willingly surrendered, every part of me.
With a flash I can see the beauty of all that I had,
As it now slips away and evades me.
Cast by my urges past, I'll never return.
I'm consumed by my poison, bound to its accelerating path unknown.
Wherever it ends, it will have taken me.
Drawn to the edge,
The fall is everything it promises to be.

I dreamed the knife would stab my heart.
Right there on the kitchen floor.
Lying on my back, awaited my desperations' moments end.
Steel's brutal truth.
Slices through its flesh, forced through bones.
It's done in an excruciating moment.
All stops in an exploding flash.
Blood drips below the boards, the crushing excise of my pain.
Pinned to the spot where my time had come.
I face the light.
And float into the vapor of those past.
My silence fulfilled.

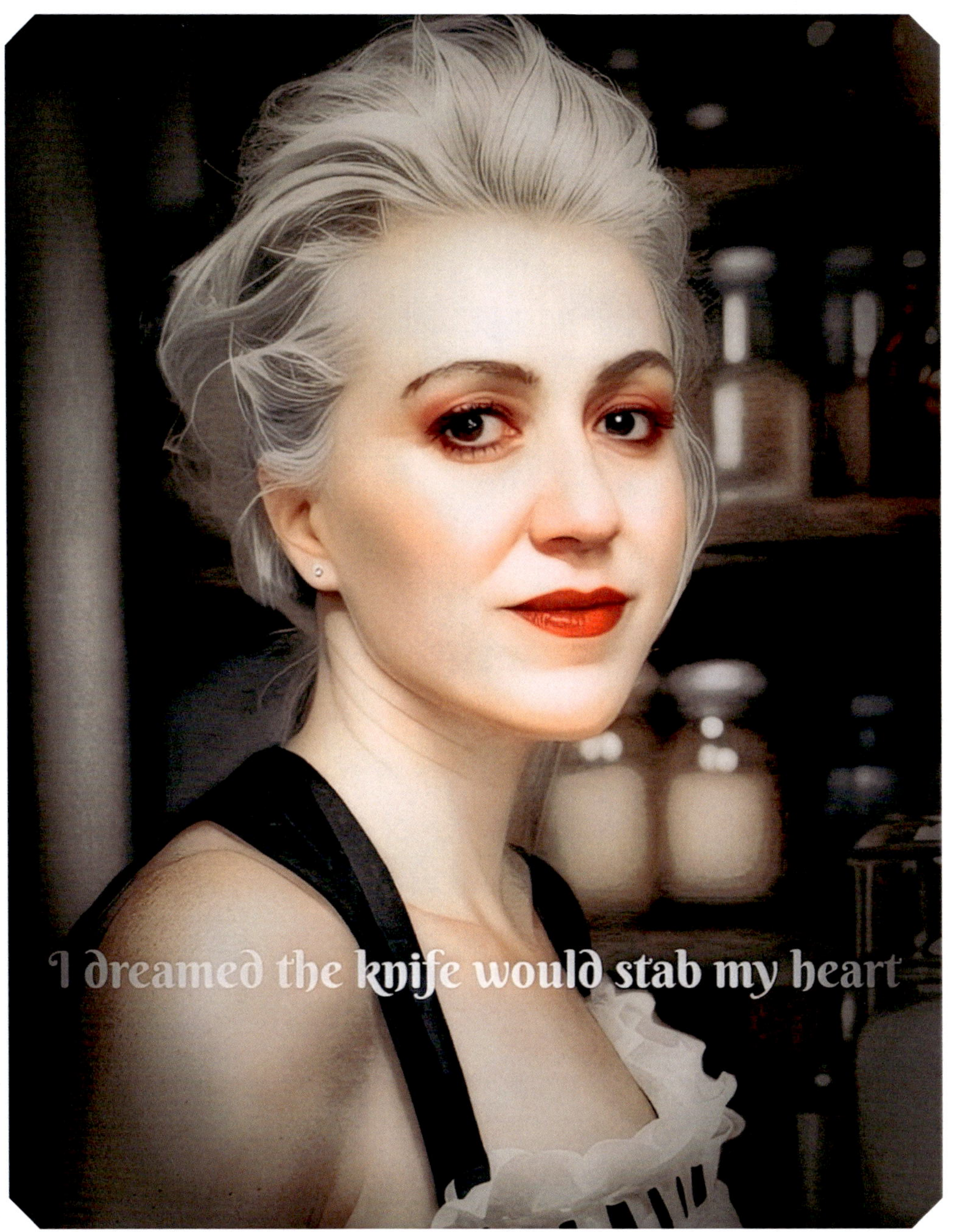
I dreamed the knife would stab my heart

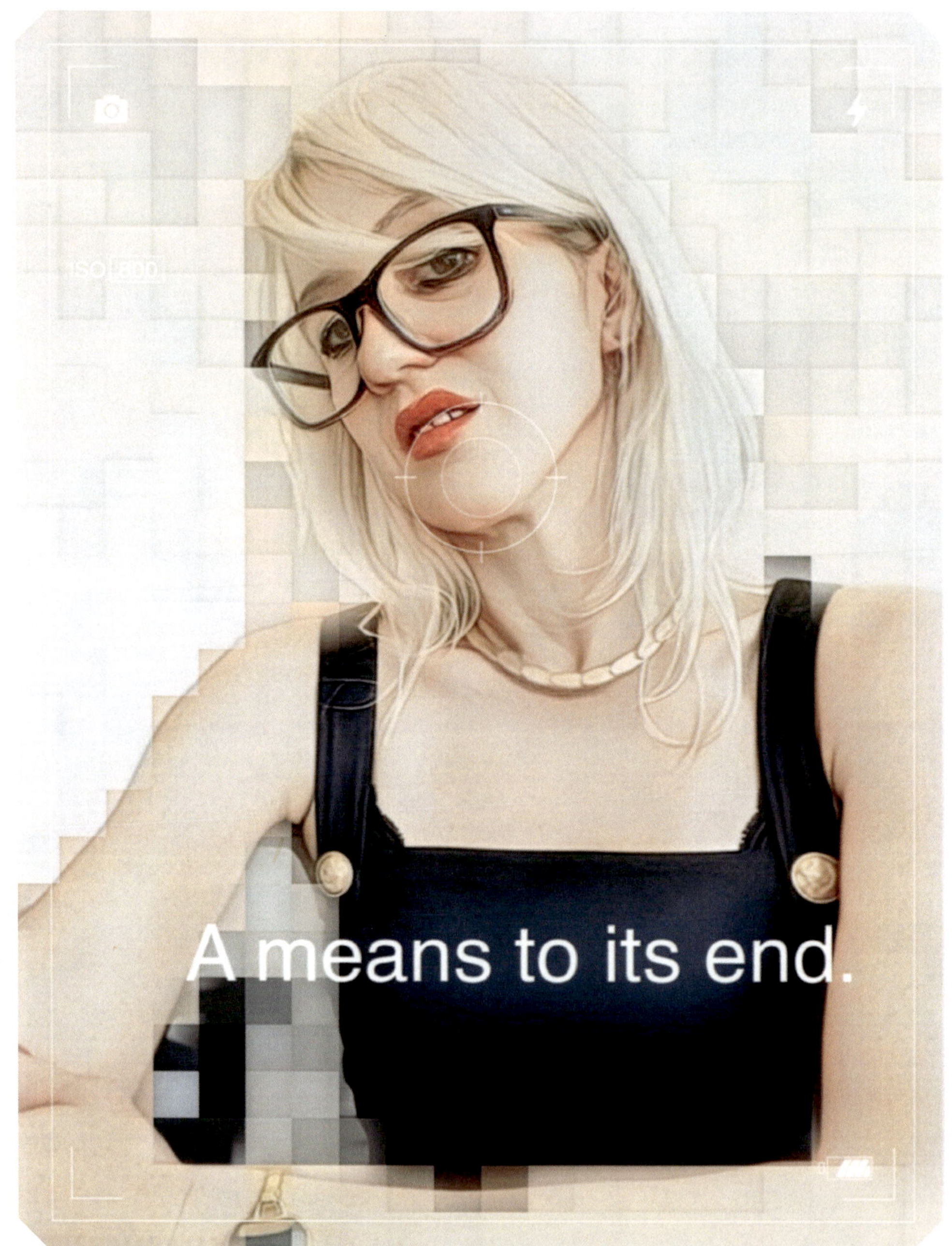
ISO 800
A means to its end.

A means to its end.
It's so clear, everything you can touch and feel.
The truths you can count on.
Skepticism is wise, swords drawn over time become yours to keep.
The holes you can pierce will lead you to truth.
The hard knowledge gained by life's midpoint,
Past disappointments come fresh and served cold.
At the table we sit, criticisms insightful flow.
Predictably right, worst outcomes best accepted.
What else but naivete, child sized fantasy should be outgrown.
Except seeing is believing means there is no belief.
Only seeing.
Irony casts shadow on the doubts that make themselves true.
Believing becomes seeing.
Dreamers ascend to life's truth.
Darkness is its own illusion made real.

I dreamed he would come.
My morning faith promises me every day,
That he is real, and one day he will come.
Mind and body at rest, I stir with the purity of my heart's love.
There is no alternative to the meaning of everything.
The reason why, there is none other.
In the brief moment when dreams and dawn collide each day,
He's there.
Right beside me, I can feel almost everything.
But with one breath closer, needing to touch, I'm awakened.
He's not there, he won't be,
Till tomorrow's dream again.
I can only pray that one day he will come.
And I'll know what it means for dreams to come true.
He'll be real and he will rescue me.
I'll never need anything more, but all inside I have to give.
To only him, all of me that comes alive.
With every passing day I wait.
My sore heart brims with hope that it's true,
That our love is real.
I dream he will come to me.
Forever and again,
I dream.

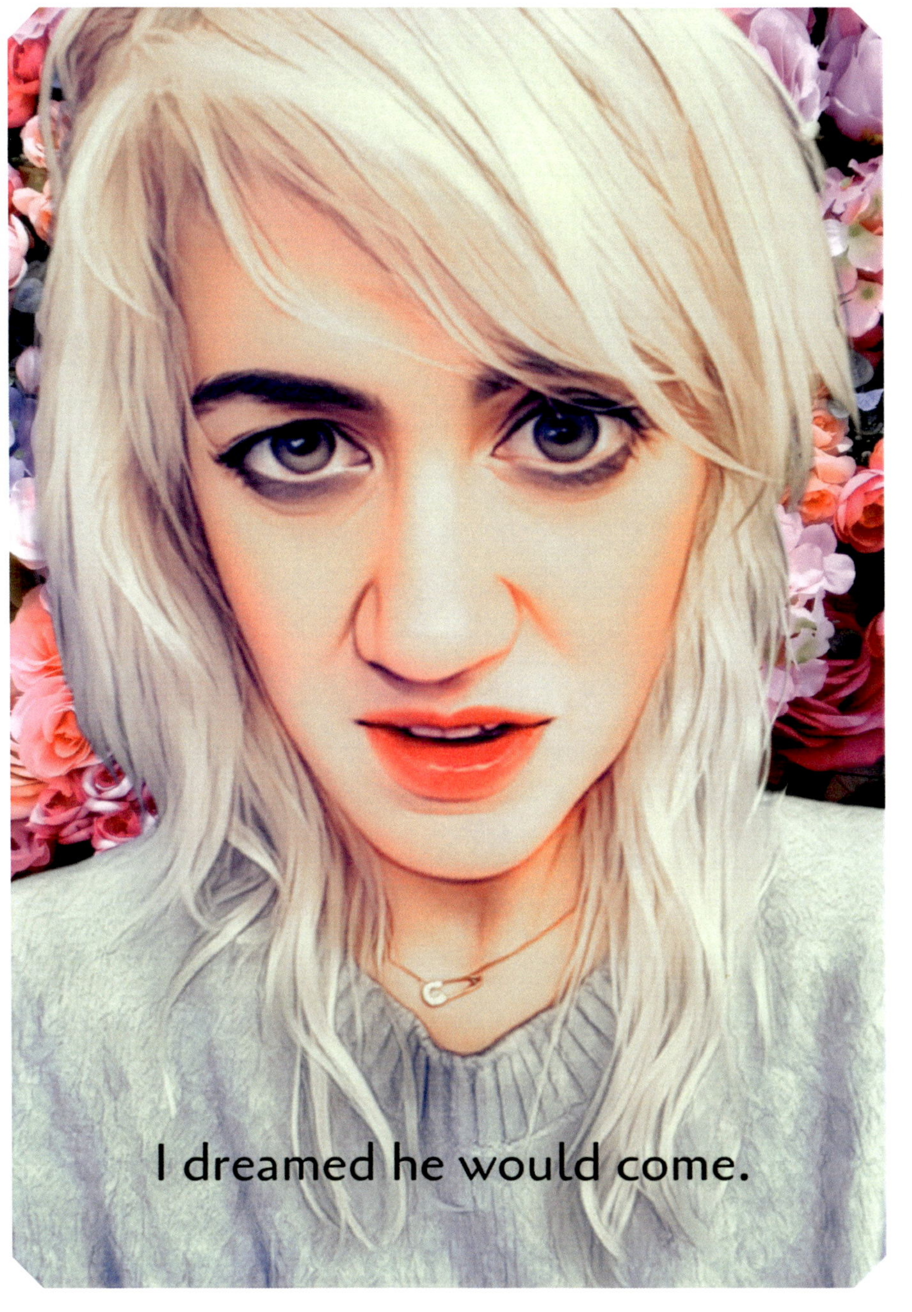
I dreamed he would come.

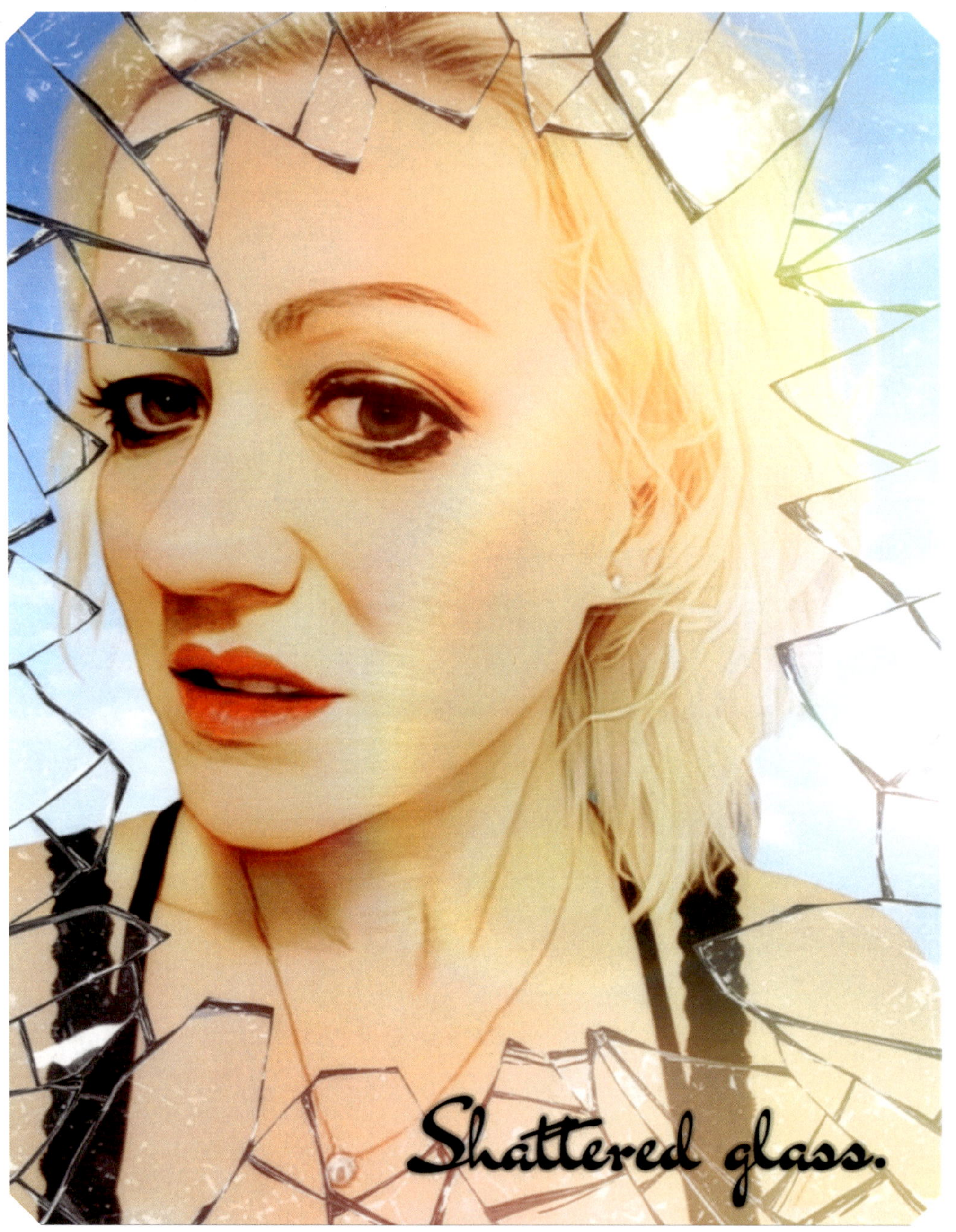
Shattered glass.

Shattered glass.
Beauty is vulnerable.
Too delicate for modern pace.
Clear and pure, it easily shatters.
Defenses of fantasy prove no match for life's force.
Wading in my treasure's pieces, I'm brought to my knees.
Over my head, blue sky and burning sun reflect a field of glare.
A flash on my skin and a glow that transcends, frame the moment.
The picture of me awash in my broken glass.
The curiosity of some, pain's exquisite when breached.
The addiction to inflict stops to stare.
I feel it cut me in a surreal moment,
How can it be? It's gone.
Shards and blood tell me it's real.
Yet its final course I replay, looping back, I always return here.
Among the jagged edges, with no other paths to choose.
Time will grind my shattered glass to glitter,
Casting light with fleeting sparkle.
It's drawn from me until I know, one day it's dust.
What I have to give, I let it cut me, without choice.
But with my heart, knowing its truth.

My blood was real.
The moment I knew my blood was real,
It was at best too late.
Times in life were everything to be,
As I was told and lived.

On the outside, the shell of me
Was everything to know.
It seemed in pace with all around.
Not a moment outside the bounds.

But inside, my blood ran true.
I held it deep within.
The feelings that were mine withheld.
Caged in my heart, not shown.

With every pace I walked life's road,
Yet one day it came to be.
My blood came forth,
Rushing through, ran free,
And saw the light of day.

In that instant,
I was gone.
In that brief moment,
I was me.

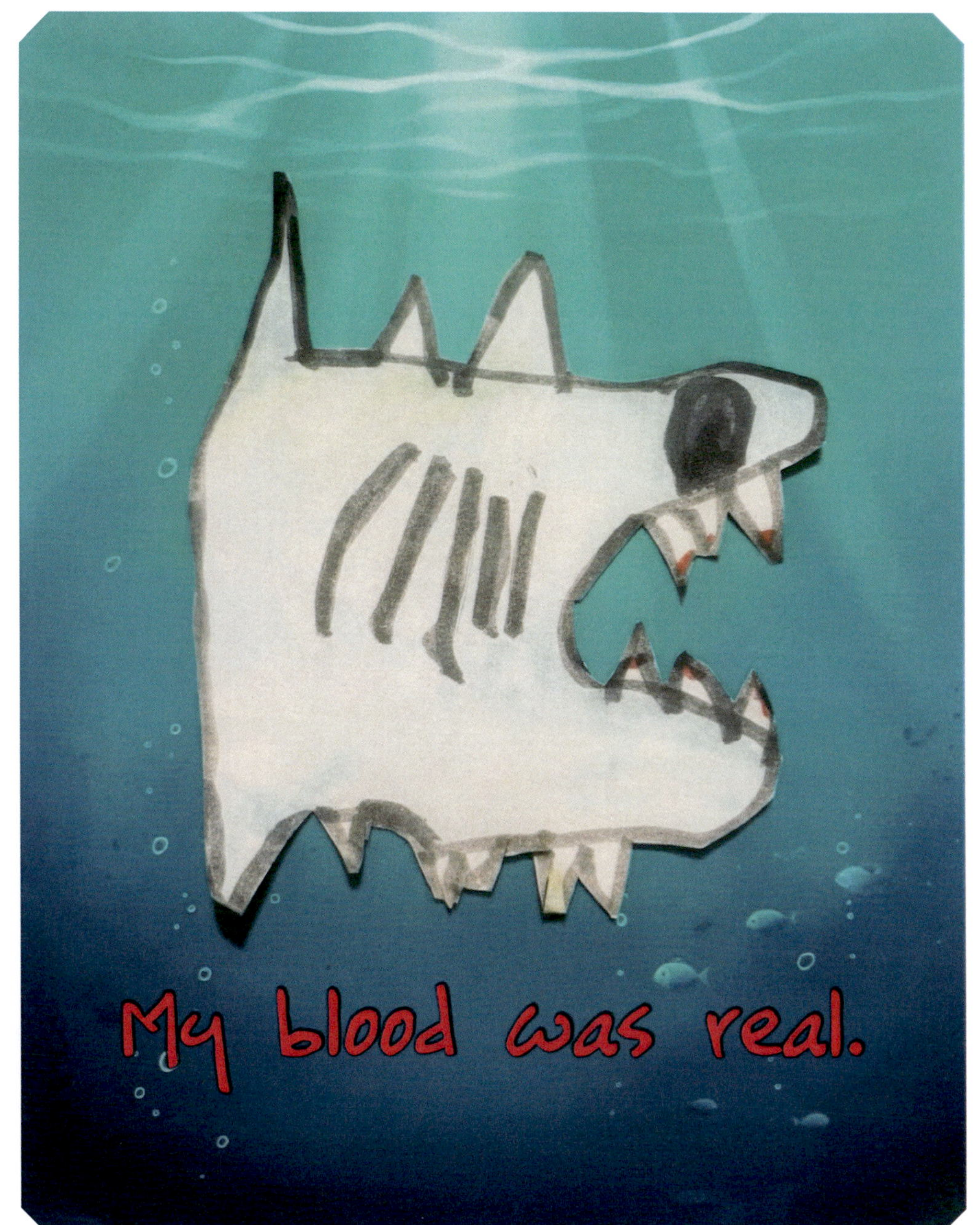
My blood was real.

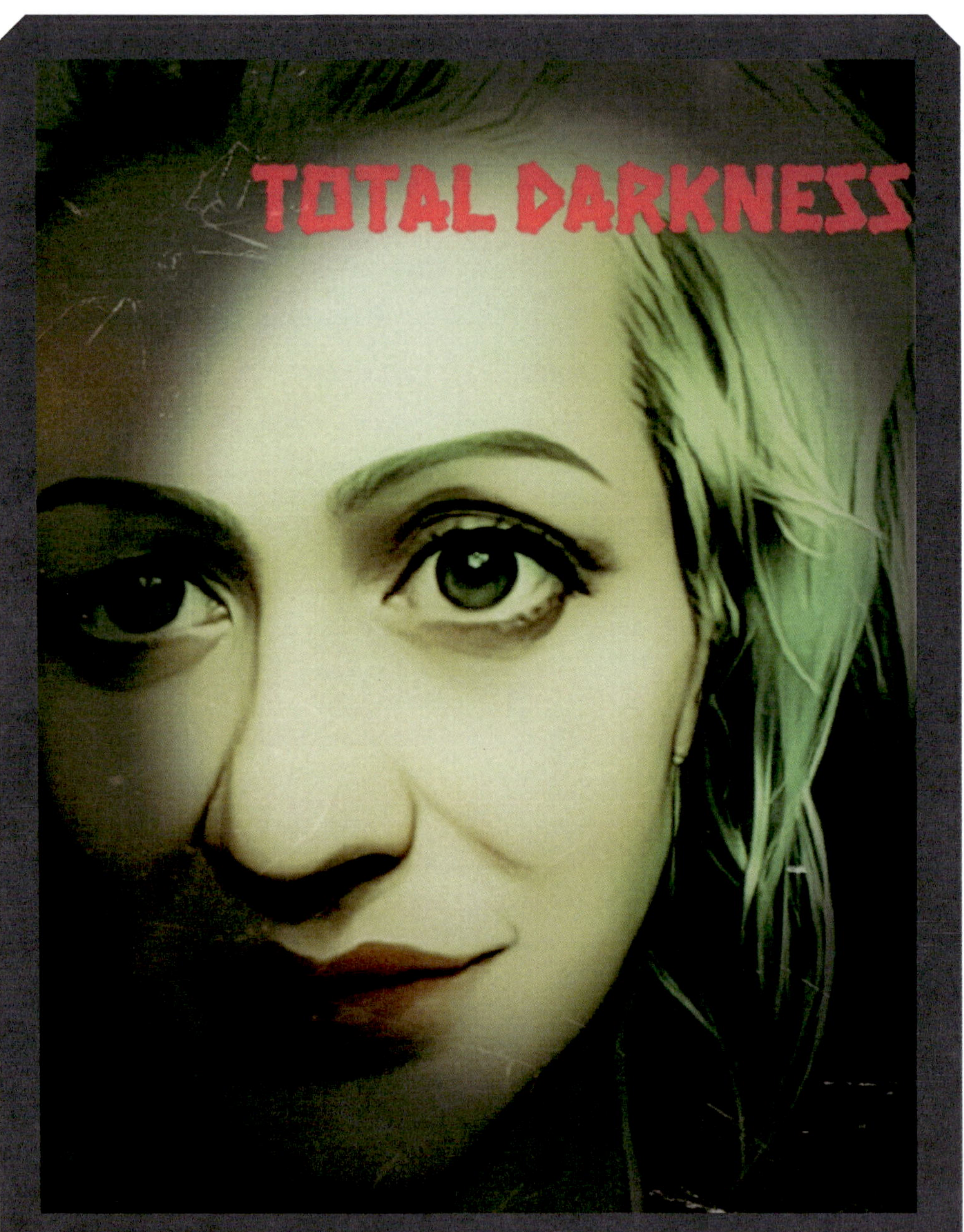
TOTAL DARKNESS

Total darkness.
In a pitch-black room,

Paralyzed by motionless darkness.

I am lost in familiarity so obscured.

Nothingness absorbs all dimensions.

My feet lose their grasp of the sinking floorboards.

Abandoned by the air,

Thick with blackness.

I am frozen in weightless suspension,

Drifting through immeasurable time.

Fear pierces my consciousness.

Unnerved by the shrillness of my own breath,

I am unable to discern the deafening silence.

An audible fragment of motion seizes me.

Breathless. Gasping.

Frenzied images torment my mind, vulnerable and exposed.

Keen and attentive,

I wait and listen.

Defenseless.

Reverberating silence.

My concentration jumbles and drifts.

Another wave of sound strikes.

Nearer, approaching.

Rushing,

Surging,

A smell,

A sensation,

An unstoppable continuous motion consumes my straining defenses.

I sense the faint hum of breathing.

Growing louder,

Nearer,

Moist heat chokes my burning throat.

Still approaching,

Unstoppable,

Growing closer,

My head is whirling,

Raging,

Pounding,

As I tumble in a bottomless darkness.

Trembling, I am startled as my powerless body strikes the wall, hitting the switch.

Illumination,

False alarm.

Follow your heart.

To follow your heart where it leads you,
Is a journey most unknown.
Faith alone travels beside you,
So many ways convinced you are lost.
You shared, awaiting adoration,
Of hearts around you, never came.
And instead face a harsh, cold darkness,
'Why can't you just be other's way?'
But to follow your heart is a life of love,
And the way you are meant to be.
With every step to lead you on,
To give yourself as destined and free.
I'll never know if I am right,
This path that I am on.
And those afraid will scold me,
With proof that I am wrong.
How I wish that you'd come with me,
Your treasured heart of grace.
Perfect as you are when in my eyes,
Not confined or bound to place.
And so I choose to follow my heart,
With the light of what can be.
Fear is not the answer.
Not for anyone, not for me.

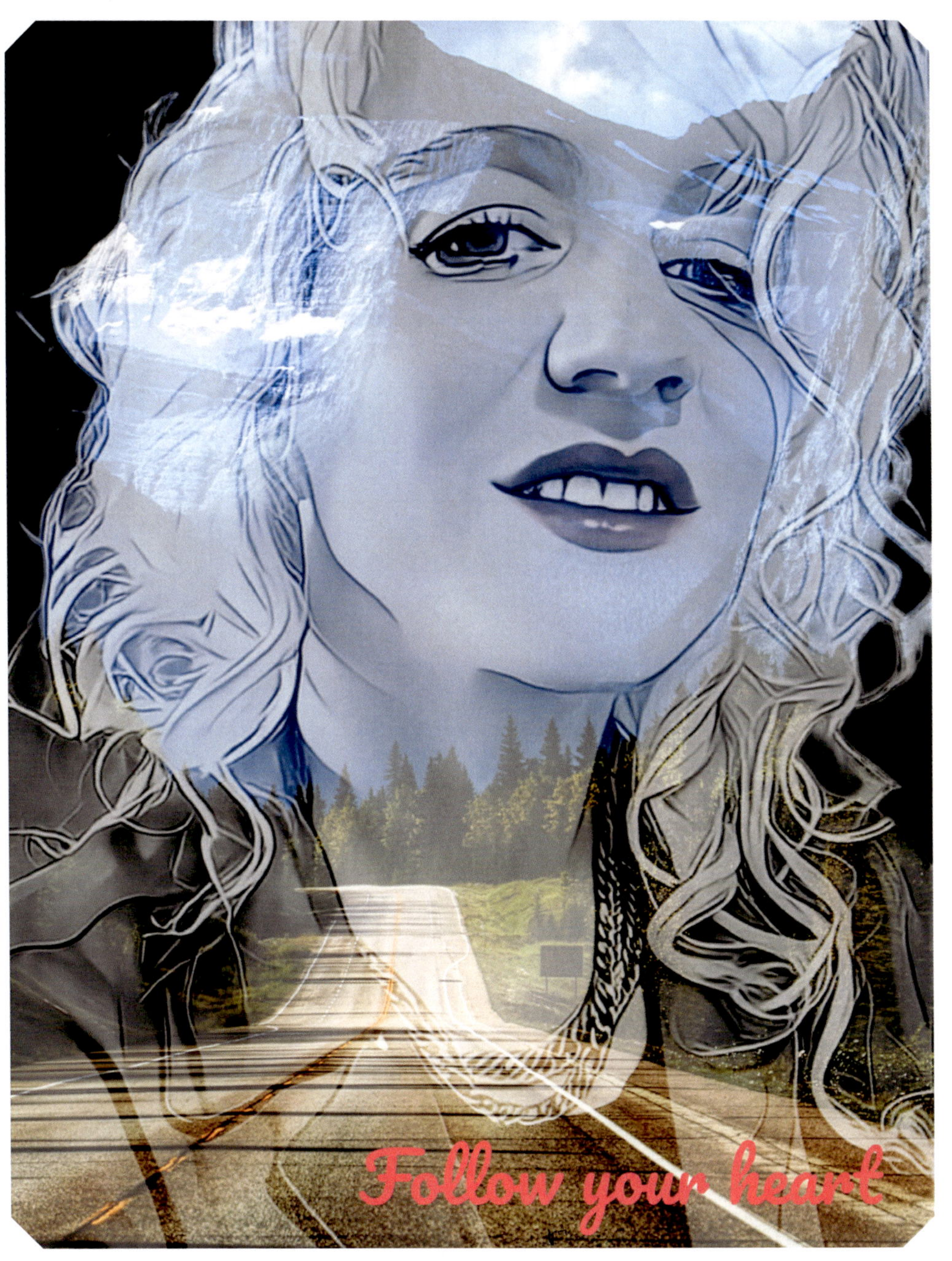
Follow your heart

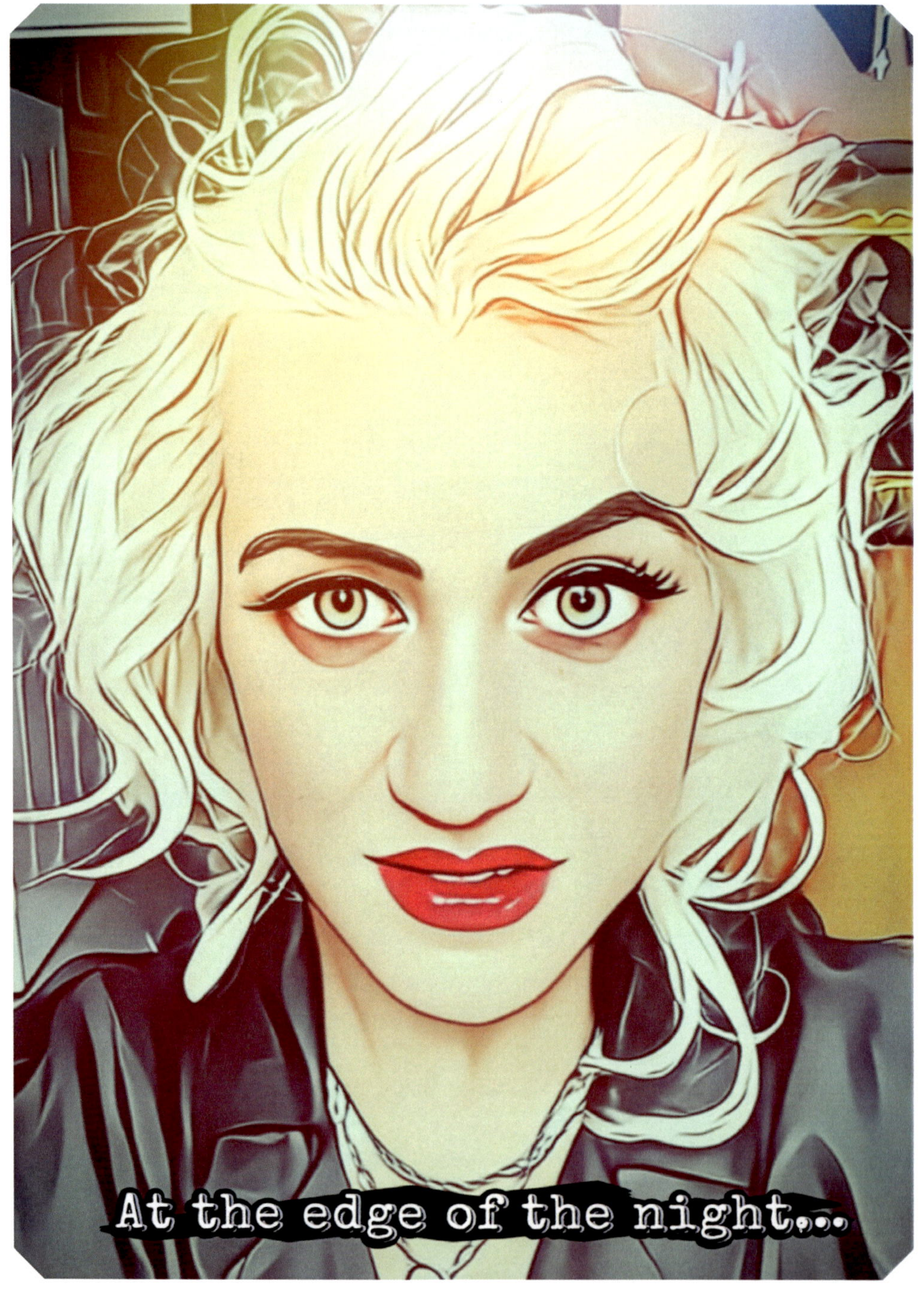
At the edge of the night...

At the edge of the night.
The edge of the night
Awaits the dawn unknown,
All possibility is breaking.
It can be yours, but not alone.
The richness of life
Is waking.

The rollercoaster.
Steady and calm,
Ease and grace,
Entered the door,
Seated in place.
Given instruction,
Told it was fine.
Turnstile's locked,
Wait, but no time.
My seatbelt is fastened,
Decision feels cursed,
I toy with the buckle,
While I'm shot with a lurch.
Body leaves spirit,
While spirit it flies.
Terror, elation,
Thrills undefined.
Joy without measure,
As I soar through brief time.
Sailing and diving
On a serpentine line.
Thrown overhead, and
Twisted towards fate.
Pushed to the limits,
But never too late.
Freed of all boundaries
While tethered to track.
My heart is
A rollercoaster,
Forever goes back.

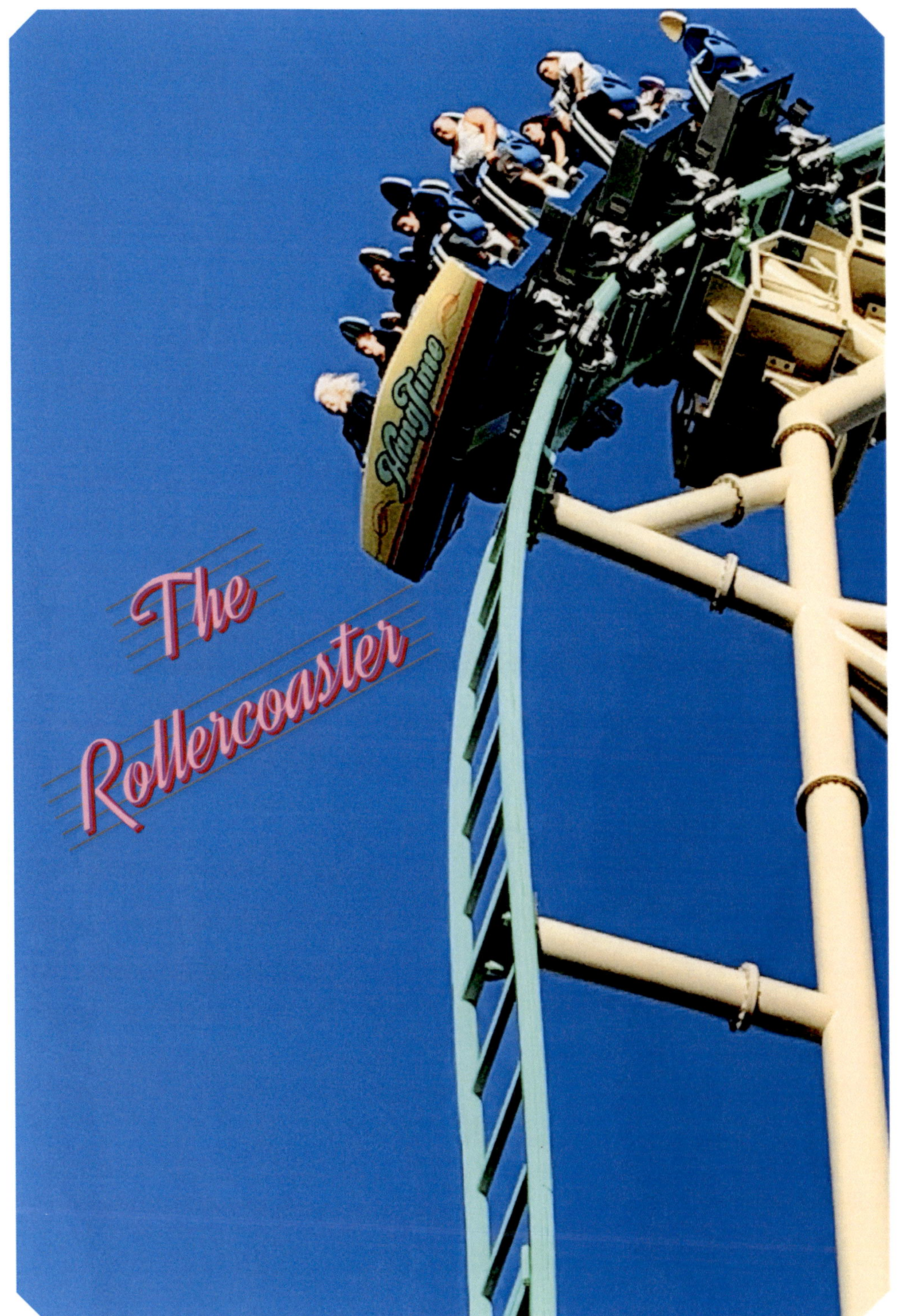
The
Rollercoaster

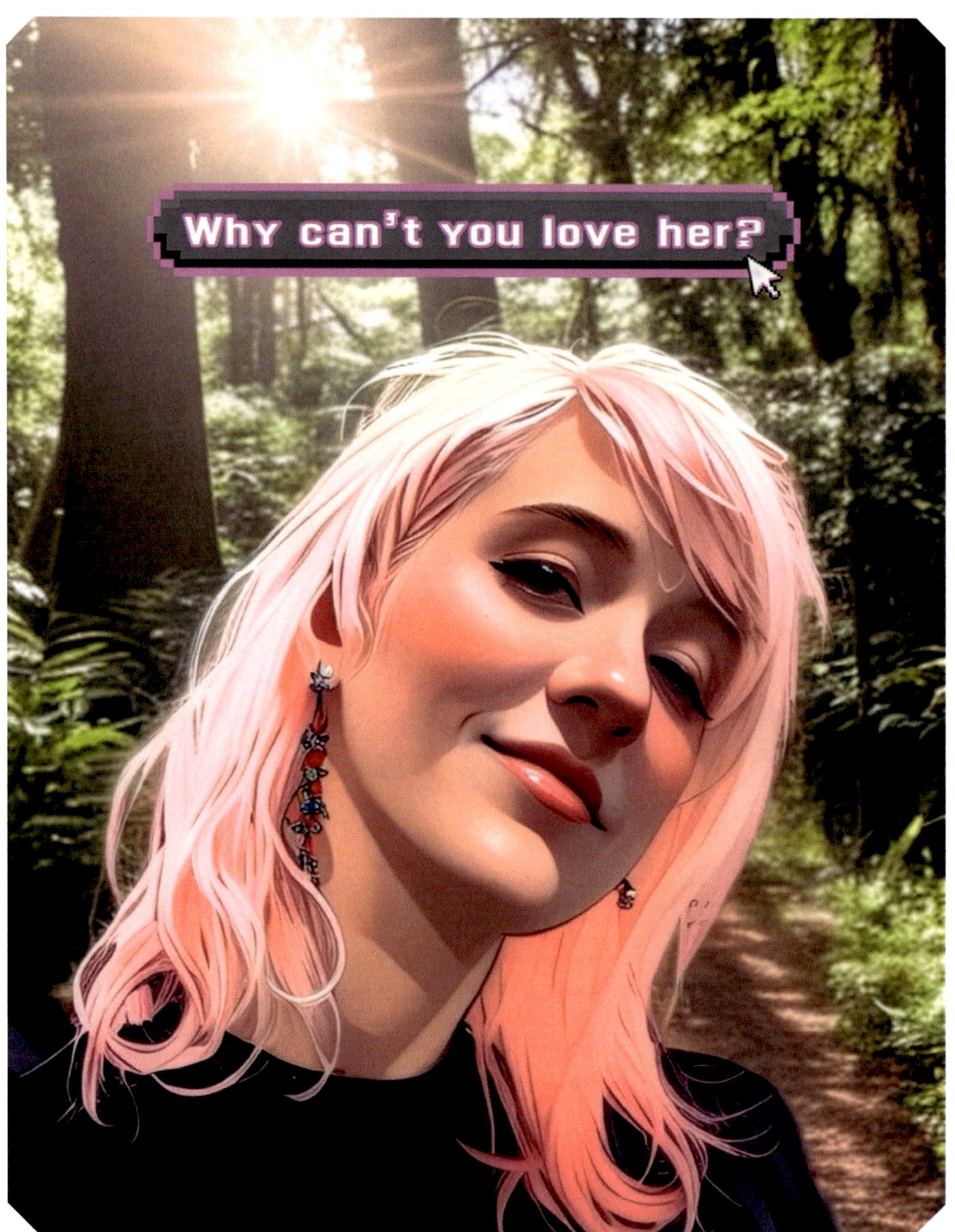
Why can't you love her?

Why can't you love her?
You're lost in her presence.
She takes your breath away.
You cannot help but look at her,
Glowing sensed,
You're warmed in every way.
You cannot believe she is real,
So much more than you had dreamed.
Can't imagine life without her,
But in this moment you're unseen.

When you finally steal her moment,
Where does respect it fly?
Why is it that she's less than?
Unworthy of meaningful time.
Why are you convinced she's harmful?
Fear invades, shadowing her grace.
Why can't she be human?
Then even more than perfectly in place.

Why is it you can't love her?
And express her beauty's worth.
Women are gifts to cherish.
Embodied in love as here on Earth.

Pushed.
Pushed beyond limits,
Trapped at the edge.
Breath swept away from me,
My body so pressed.
The walls appear everywhere,
Closed on all sides.
Clawing with fingernails,
But caught deep inside.
The plaster is peeling,
The air stale and thick,
My emotions are toxic,
And making me sick.
There's no one to listen, and nowhere to go.
I could scream but I gasp
As I'm choked by my throat.
Running fingers on surface to pull the alarm.
My world is on fire, beyond any to charm.
Hope becomes hopeless, as it all feels too late.
It's so overwhelming,
Confronting my fate.
My way is not welcome, and I tried to escape.
But now they have found me, seething anger to sate.
Pushed till I'm broken, I fall to the ground.
No one is coming, and nothing profound.
There can be no exception to the rules how they play.
I can live and accept it,
Or shall it all end this way.

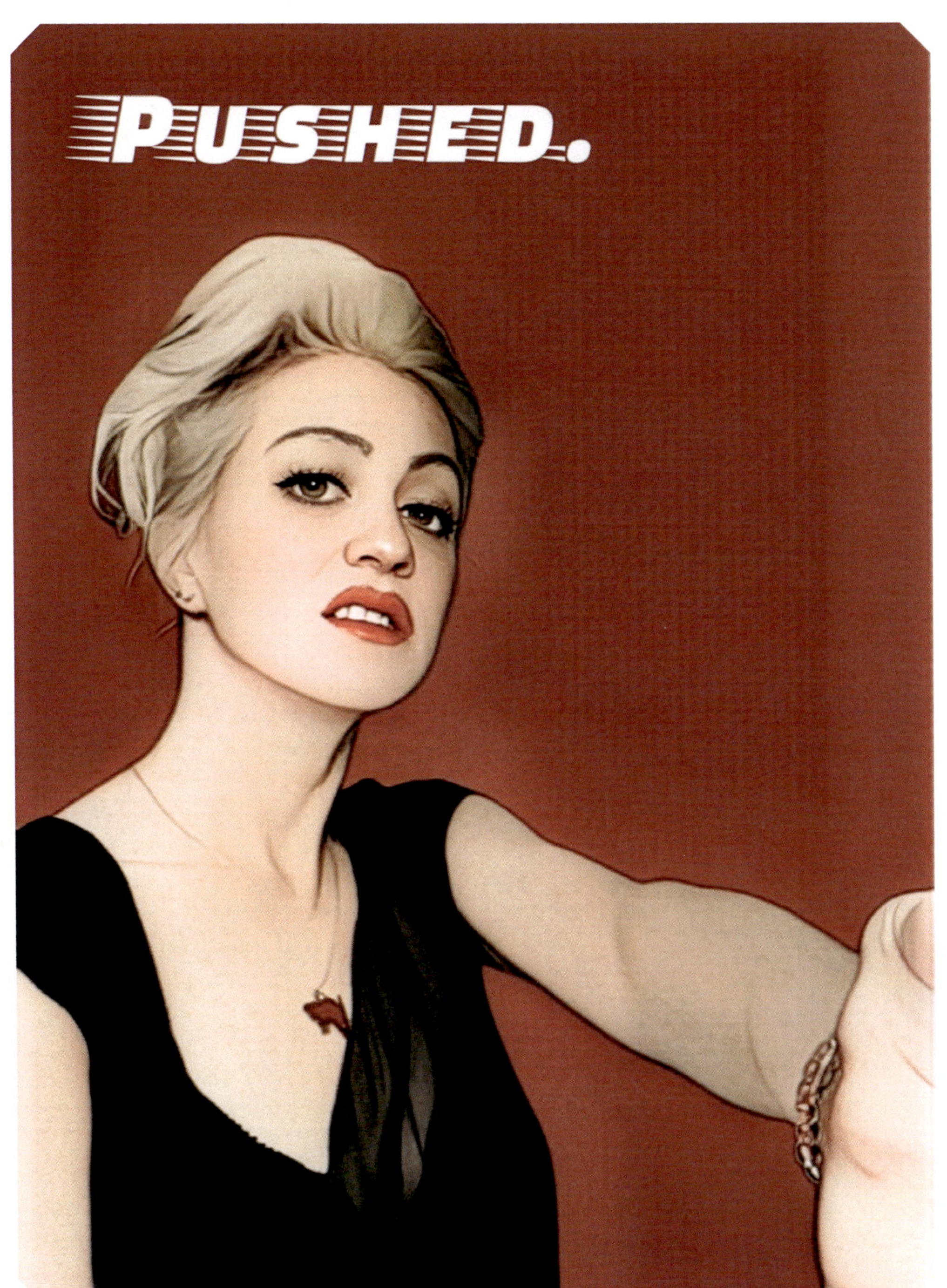
PUSHED.

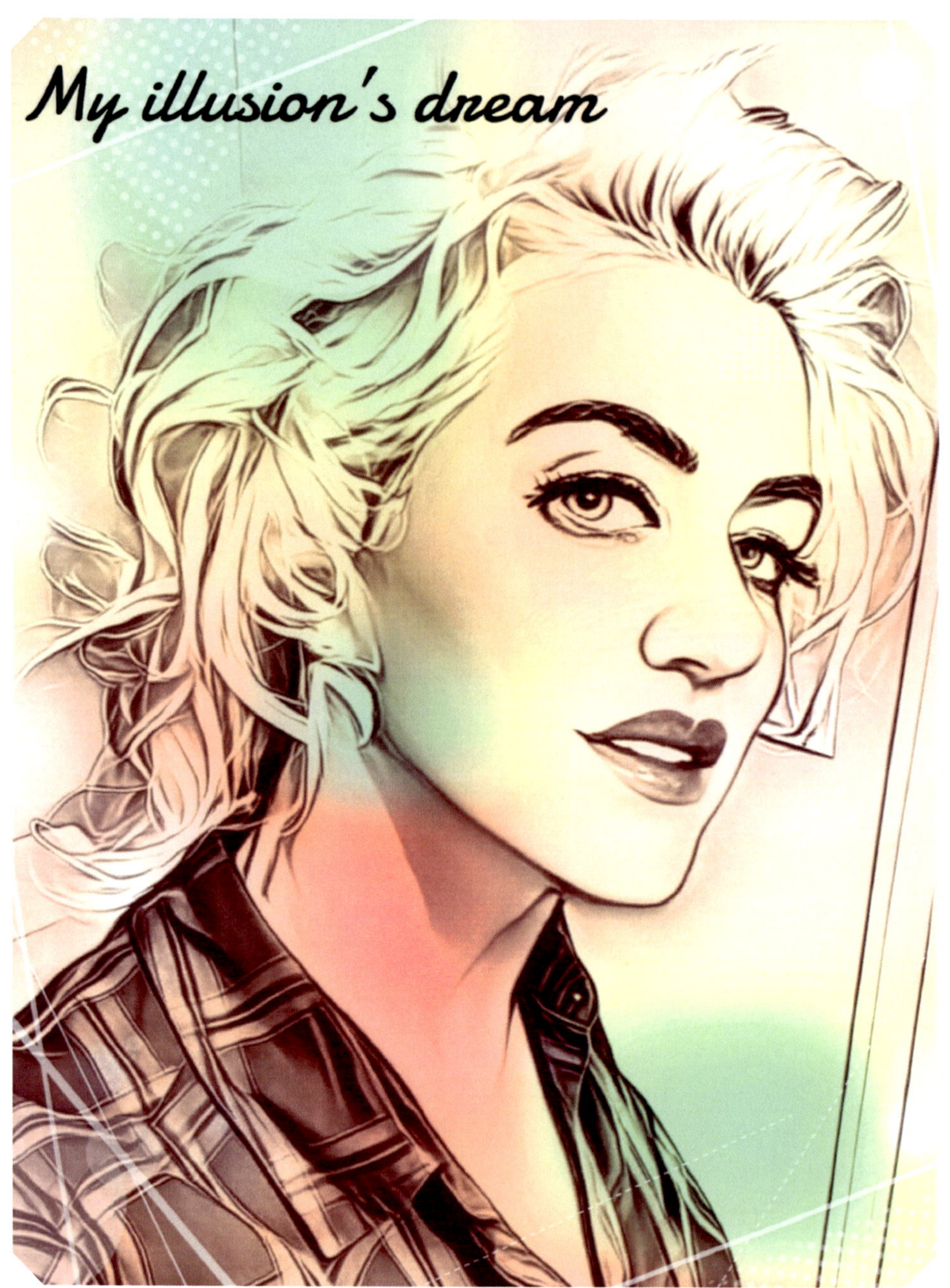
My illusion's dream

My illusion's dream.
I imagined what could be.
Saw it as real.
Know that it's better,
The love that I feel.
Too hard to accept it,
That none of it's true.
My dream an illusion,
With pain as my proof.

Your hand in mine.

If I could go back to the moment
When I first held your hand in mine,
How I sensed that we would forever be,
Beating in each other's hearts.
Like nothing that I knew before,
And between us as could only be,
The magic of our journey beyond,
Adventures grand as you and me.
Time went on and moments came.
Fire and ice of times we spent,
Could only ever deeply forge
What we share, our spirits bound.
The light that glows behind my eyes
And warms my heart when I think of you.
How times of wonder made anew
Everything that could be.
Corners then unknown, revealed,
Turning round changed life forever.
Dark skies in hard times, pierced with love,
Prevailing stronger than the storm.
As I can go back in time,
To the moments I held your hand in mine,
And have you with me then.
You're etched in my heart deep within.
Wherever then in life you go, forever we will always be,
Your hand in mine and mine in yours,
Together.

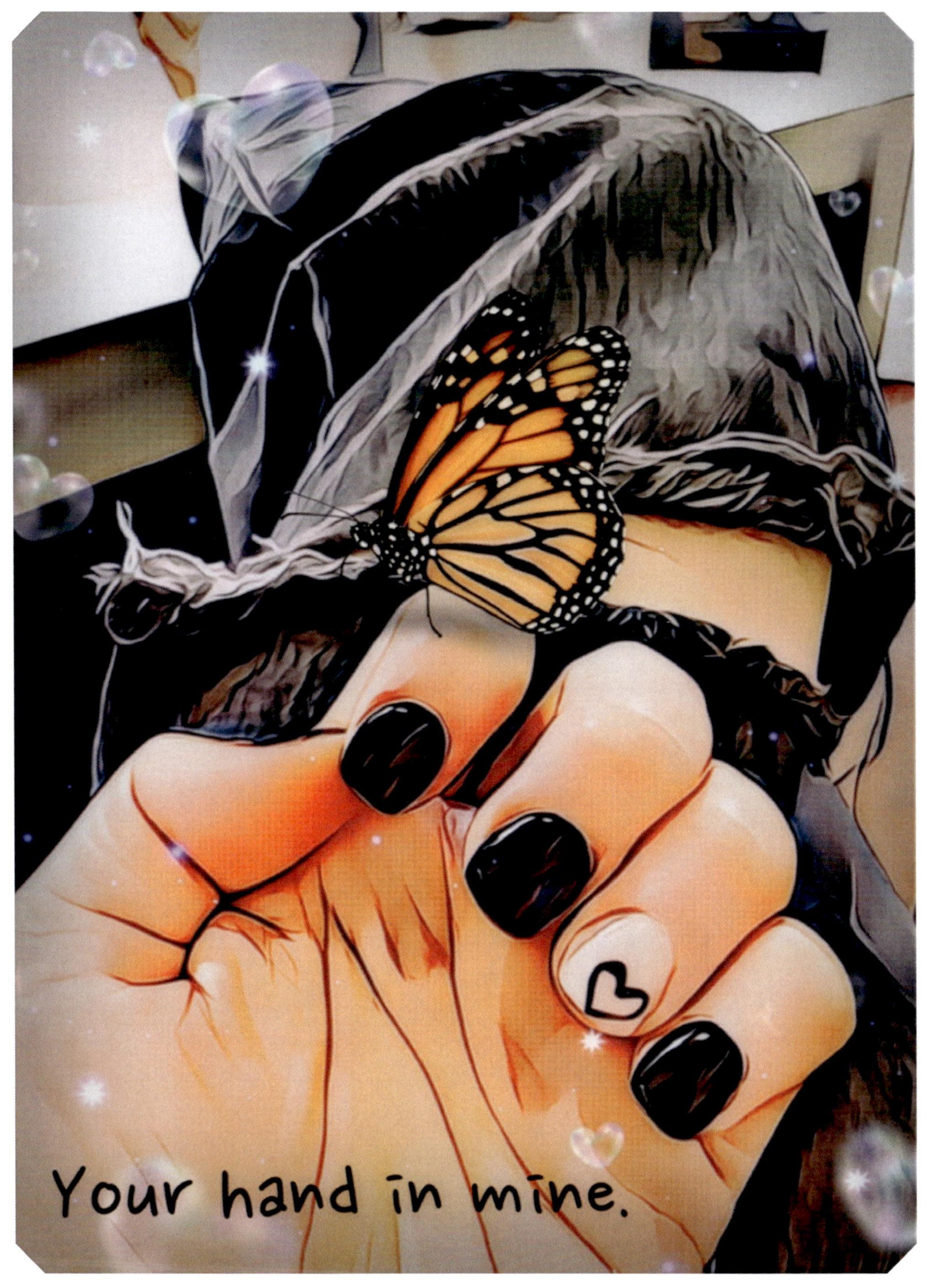
Your hand in mine.

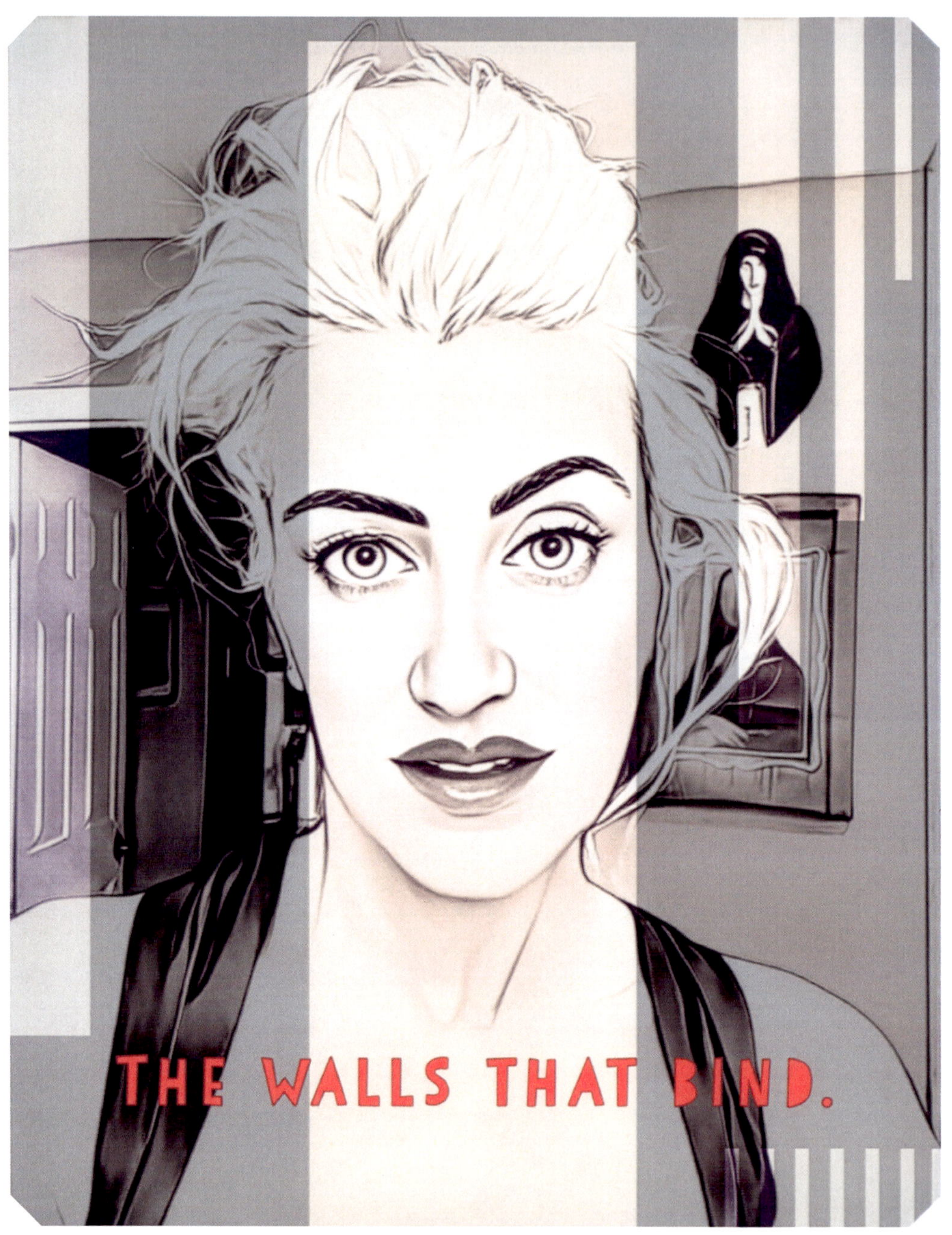
THE WALLS THAT BIND.

The walls that bind.
An invisible wall
Kept me from you
While seated by your side.
Nothing to do could tear it down,
But strain inside my mind.
The wash of my tears couldn't wear its hold
As time strengthened the glass.
And how I wished to sense you near
Empty silence that wouldn't pass.
Slowly all slipping away from me,
Trapped helpless, left to fade.
In my barrier's clutch I stared alone,
As once familiar space now evades.
These walls we have do break us down
And erase life's precious touch.
Without beating hearts a stale, cold place,
Breeds isolation and nothing much.
Our walls do not keep goodness in
But keep all promise out.
The future is to share much more,
Not learn to live without.
With great hope I have a second chance
To hear without loss or pain.
And with this prayer for forgiving trust,
This wall won't stand again.

Deep in the well.
Upon great sadness I tumbled,
Endlessly falling,
My downward spiral like a dream.
Reaching the bottom I landed,
Resting upon moist, deep earth.
From far above, sunlight cascades down,
Illuminating bright green shoots,
Pressing through the rich soil underneath, and all around me.
Down upon the basin's floor
Warmth is so fleeting.
As the angle's glow finds me,
In a tranquil moment of hope.
Somehow this tender new grass,
So frail but alive, can by its future promise
Spring to life in this dark, hollow place.
With my hands around my knees,
My tears transformed in their substance,
As newborn innocence reveals its purity's strength.
Deep in the well
In this time of despair,
Shedding pain's past and embracing my heart,
I am too, reborn.
Rising once more,
As new life now begins.

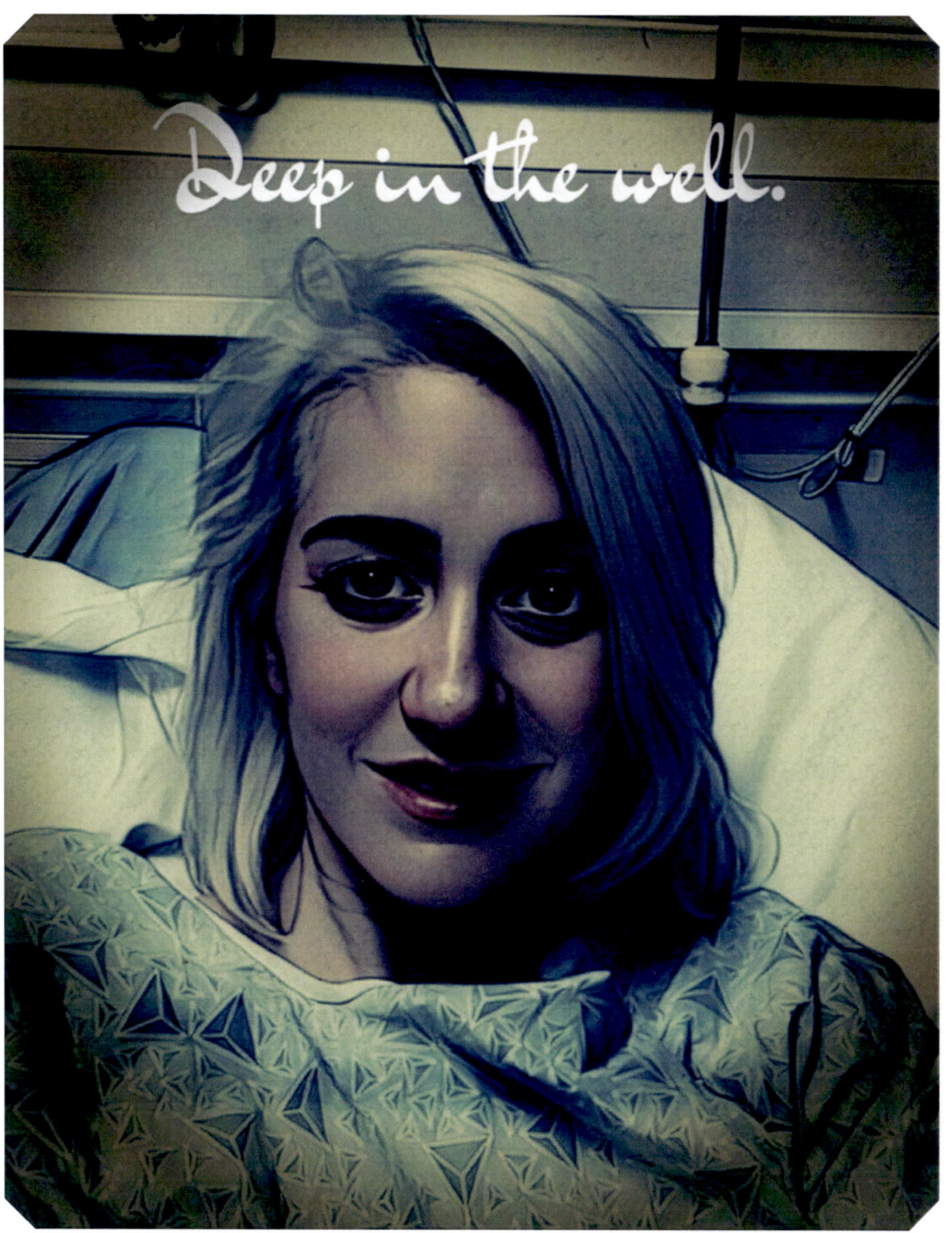
Deep in the well.

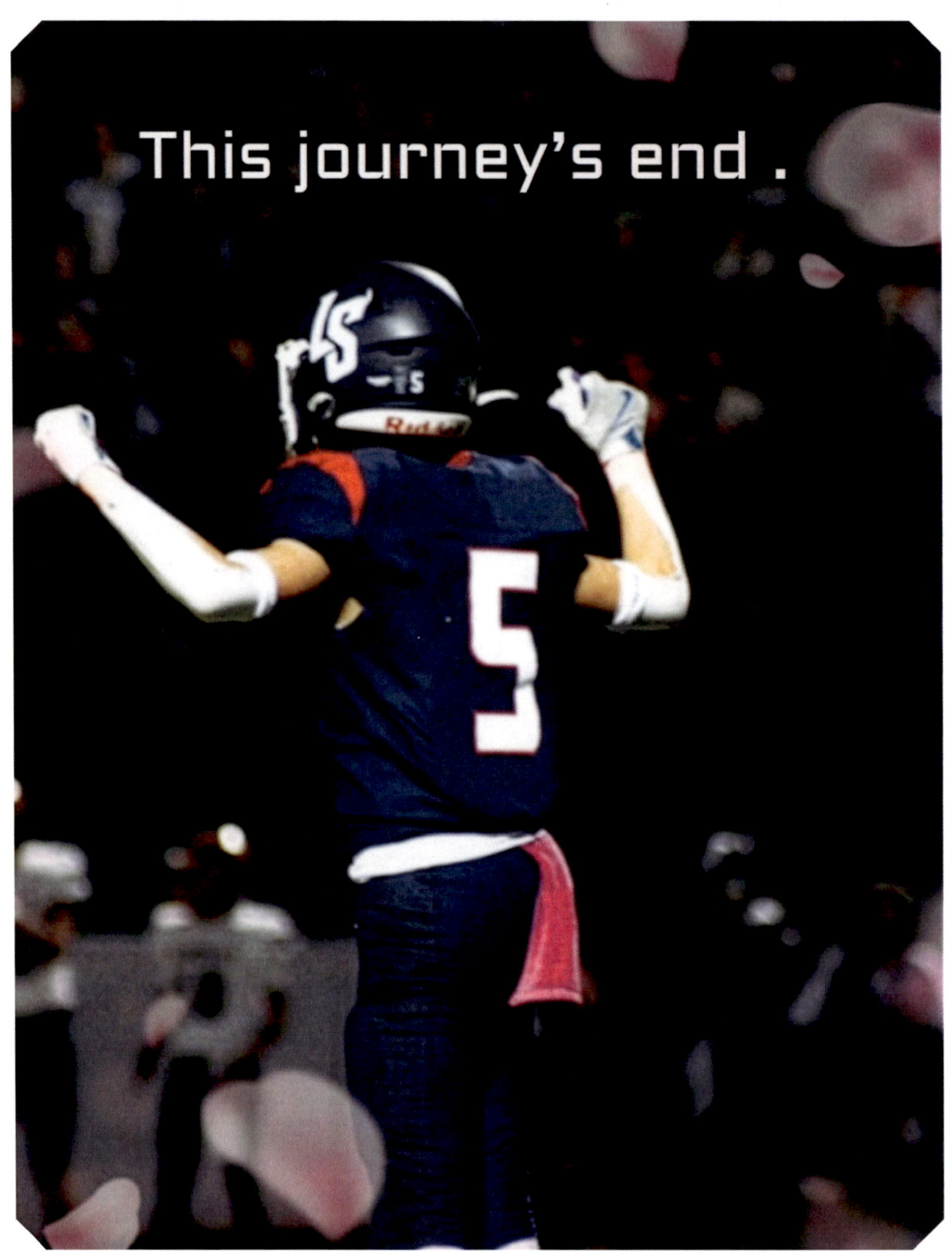
This journey's end .

This journey's end.
Within these fleeting moments, I find myself
At another year's end.
The glistening lights sparkle, echoes of joy surround me,
The fire's warmth burns the chill of brisk air.
Just as the long winter shadows whisper
Of what this year will leave behind,
Having reached its journey's end.

The dance of light in the darkness
Tells the tale a thousand years old and many more.
Spirits of the memories that live inside us,
Move and shift within us, and glow in our eyes.
Our hearts fueled through generations, sharing life's road.
Knowing each end will always be,
For all who bear witness to the morning's break,
The dawn of each new beginning.

With grateful hope of travels to be told,
May the future filled with promise begin anew.
Bittersweet, as we gaze at the crossroads,
Upon the fading sunset's bright green flash,
At this journey's end.

There has never been us.
This moment that has never been.
Time that we now stand within.
Our gaze beyond the vista's crest.
There has never been us.
Lights ablaze cast round our frame.
Our shadows boldened by our gait.
The purpose clear upon us now.
We carry on with solemn vow.
That never this treasured instant held
Ever be forsaken.
With great risk thrust we know our task.
Stakes all or nothing we must pass.
Our hearts with true purpose brim,
With every tool we need to win.
Love and justice will prevail
As evil's frailty sets to fail.
And from the wreckage our hopes to raise
Every soul to higher ground.
No wasted words, we know our cause.
Our unity bonds but every flaw.
In our lifetimes spent we're called to might.
On this dark precipice we are the light.
These are the days; this is our time.
There has never been us.

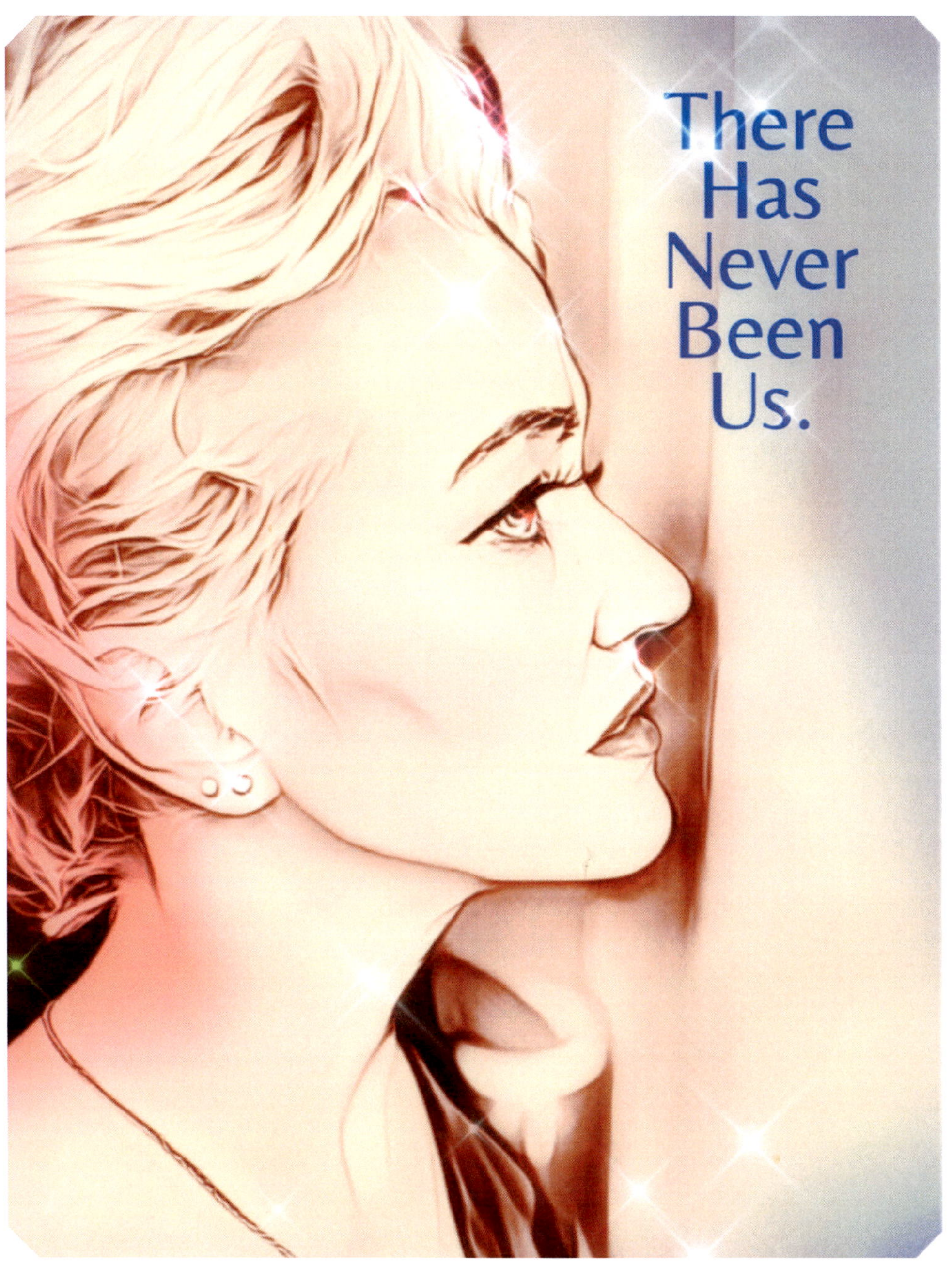
There
Has
Never
Been
Us.

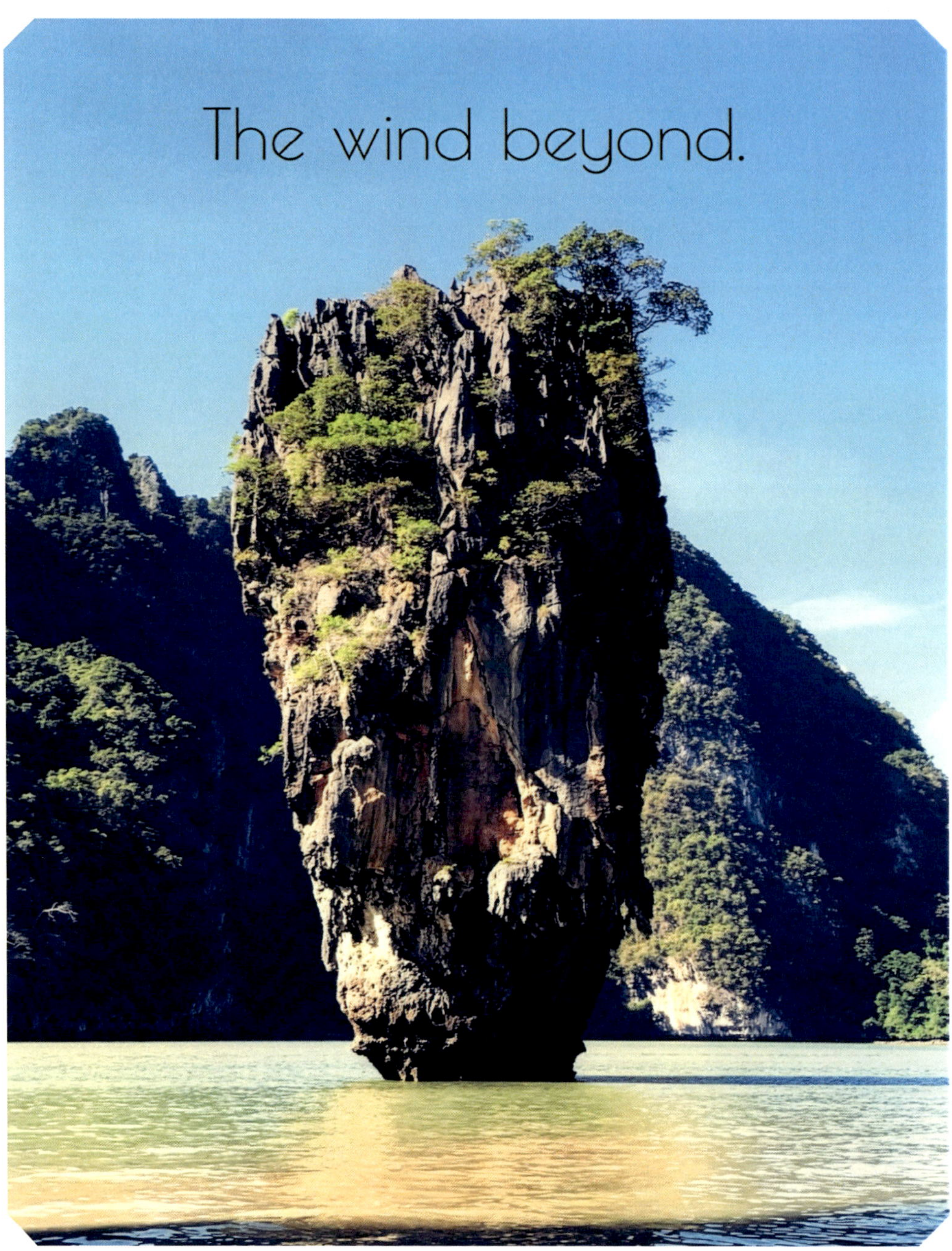
The wind beyond.

The wind beyond.
Lifted up, I rose
And sailed away.
With the wind beyond
I traveled one day.
My feet rested at last
Upon firm ground.
The world was new,
Both lost and found.

The air's rich flavors of spices sweet.
Nothing I knew could find repeat.
I closed my eyes, and all seeped in,
Every last wonder of time within.
This space so vast with treasures told
Moments unconfined and newly bold.

I grew to love my discovery's gifts
Yet could never be the place I missed.
Returning home, I carried my pack.
Graced by air so fresh, no turning back.
With the breath of the wind, in new time I leap.
The feeling beyond was mine to keep.

The crossing.
In time I knew
I would come here.
With great reserve, me feet pressed to the cross.
So fearful to change, my heart like a weight bound to my legs.
Everything I know lies ahead on the straight path before me,
Diving into the horizon.
And with that,
I turn.

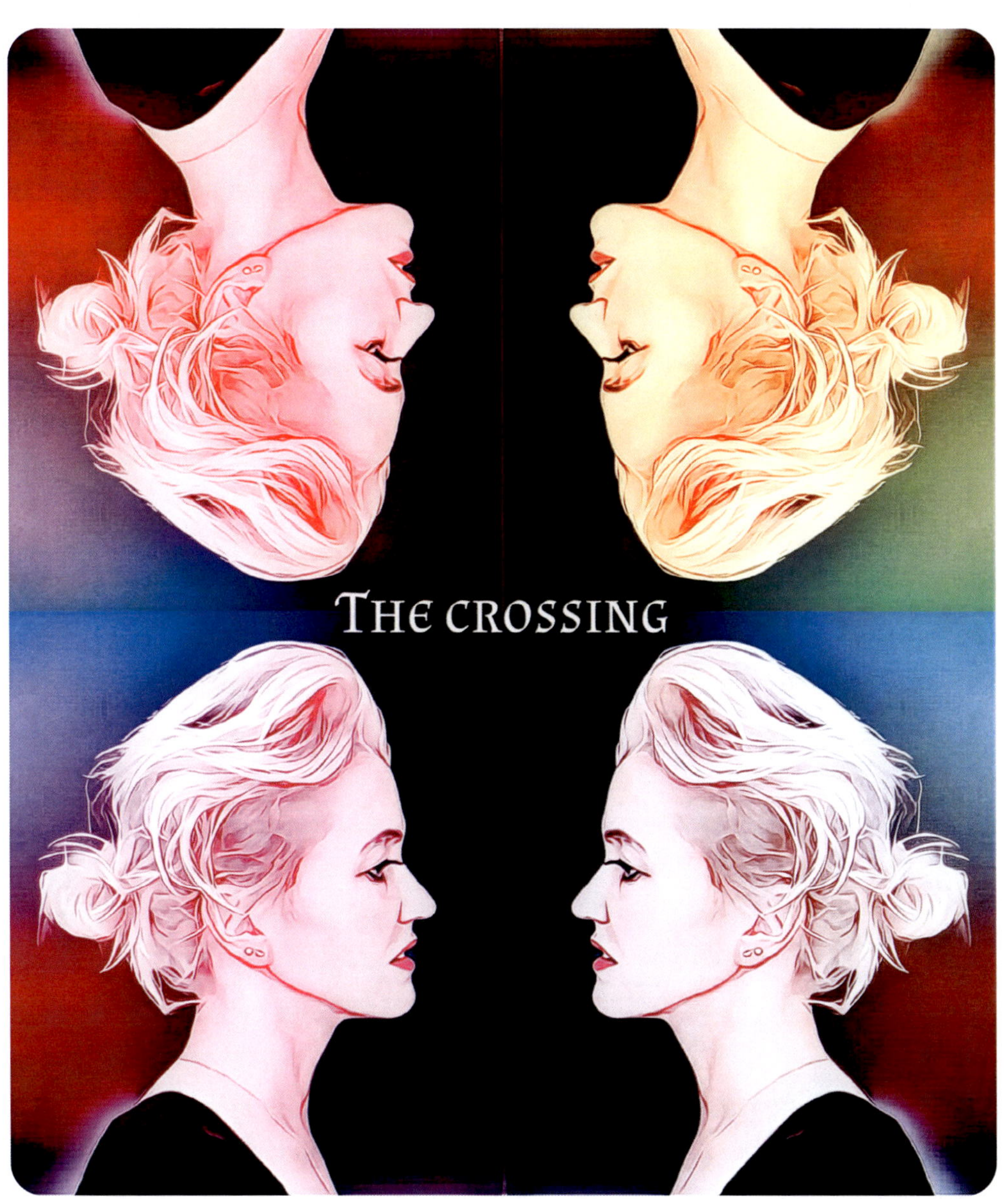
THE CROSSING

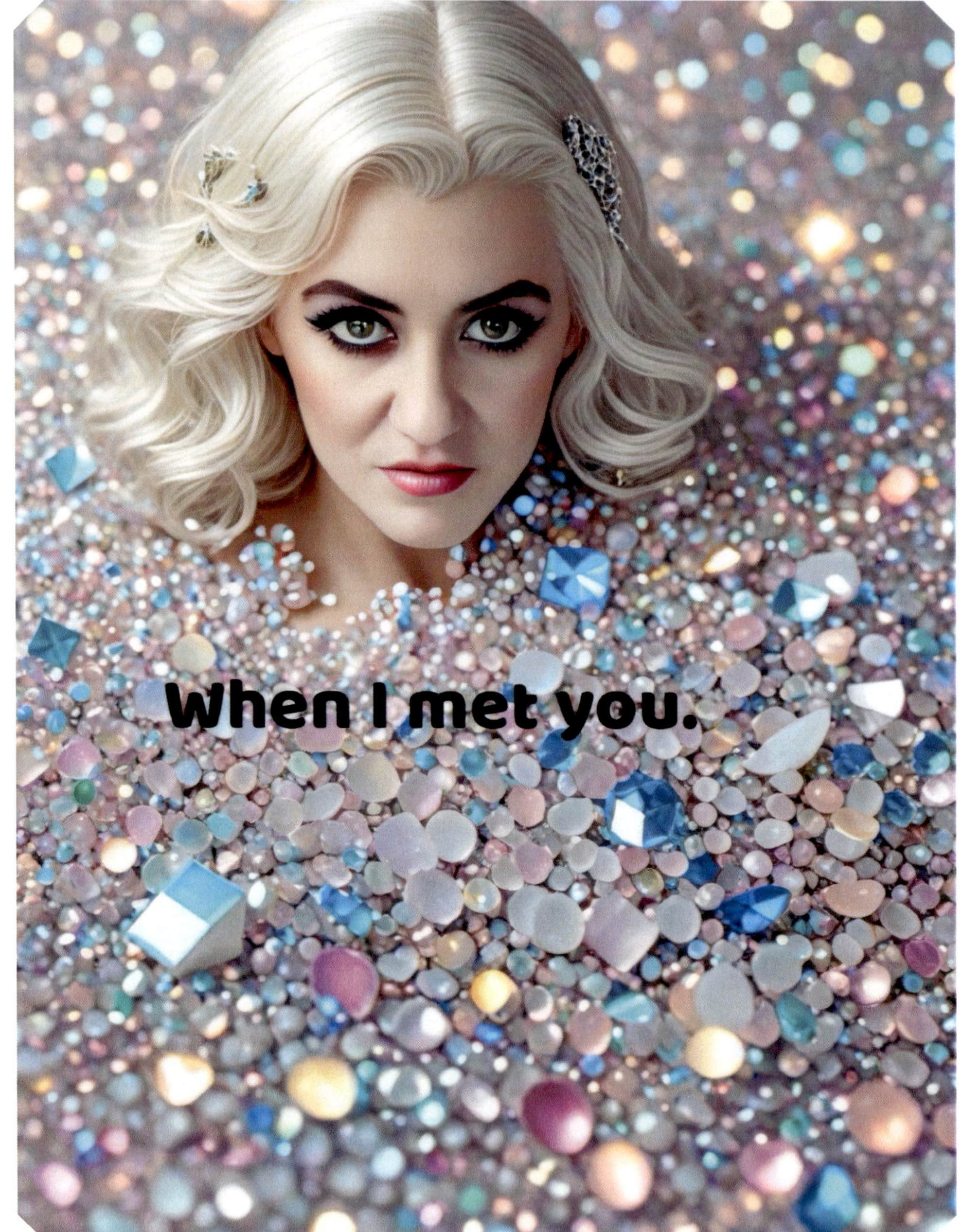
When I met you.

When I met you.
My heart was full.
When I held you,
My self, complete.
When I'm with you,
My world has changed.
Since you came,
My life feels new.
Such wistful hope,
Which I never knew to dream,
Becoming possible.
How I wish you would stay,
And that you feel the same.
We will have each other,
In every way,
To fall in life,
In love,
Together, with you.

The wall that I find.
Or shall I say it finds me.
Funny so familiar
Yet never knowing,
Where it will be.
I try to break through, and I think I'll slip past.
My first steps so tenuous,
As I pray it will last.
But its presence too strong.
It's built to keep.
It's built to entrap me,
Impressed to stand deep.
Its shadow it darkens the light of my gaze.
I feel I succumb to the frame that pervades.
In my life I've been told,
I've been made to believe,
That its presence invisible,
The world at my feet.
Those words now feel empty.
The stone cold to touch.
The faces are shallow,
The message without.
It towers before me,
So I shift around.
I smile like I mean it,
While crushed by my doubt.
Yet all I can hope as I do every day,
May its hold fade and crumble,
To feel free on my way.

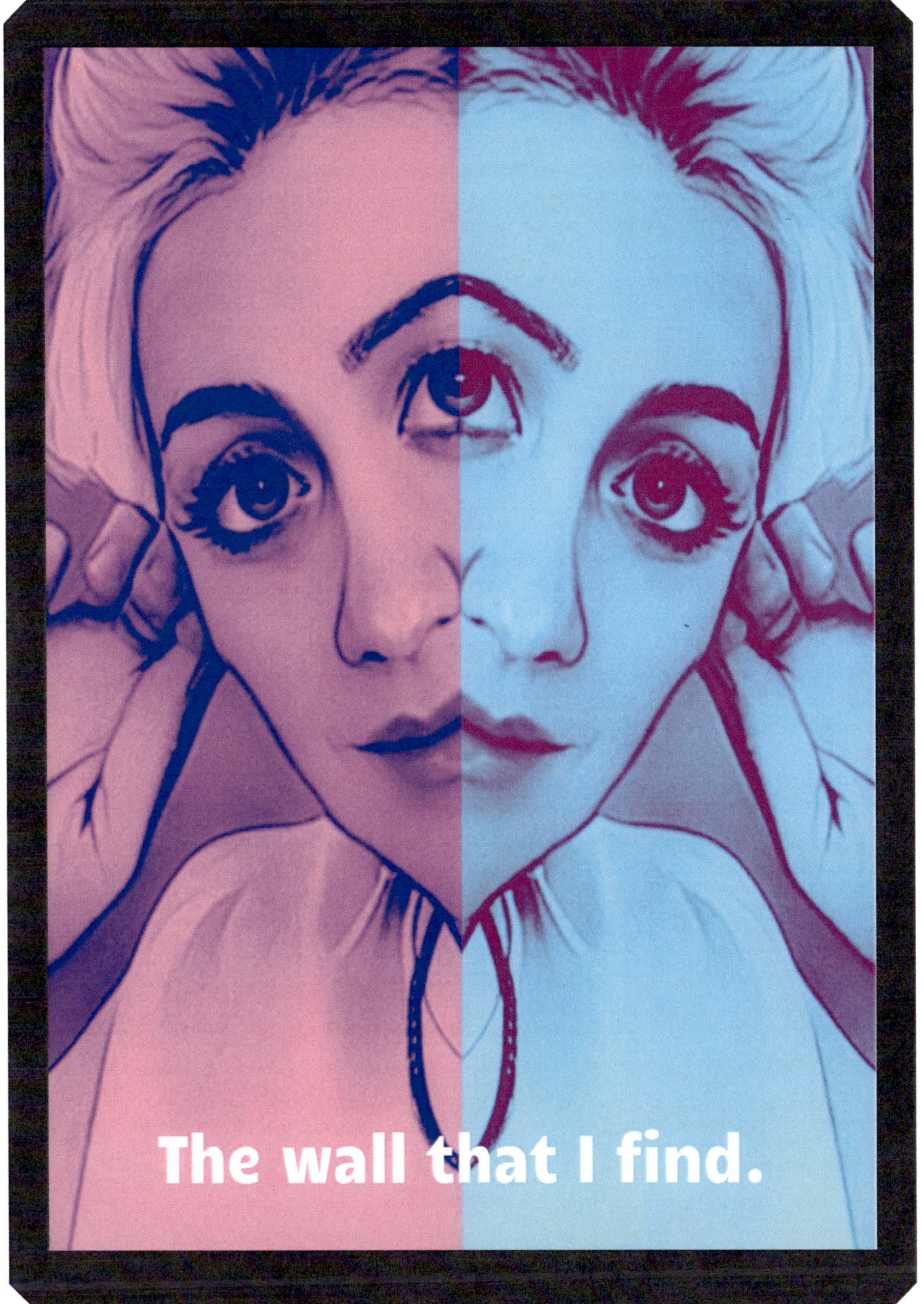
The wall that I find.

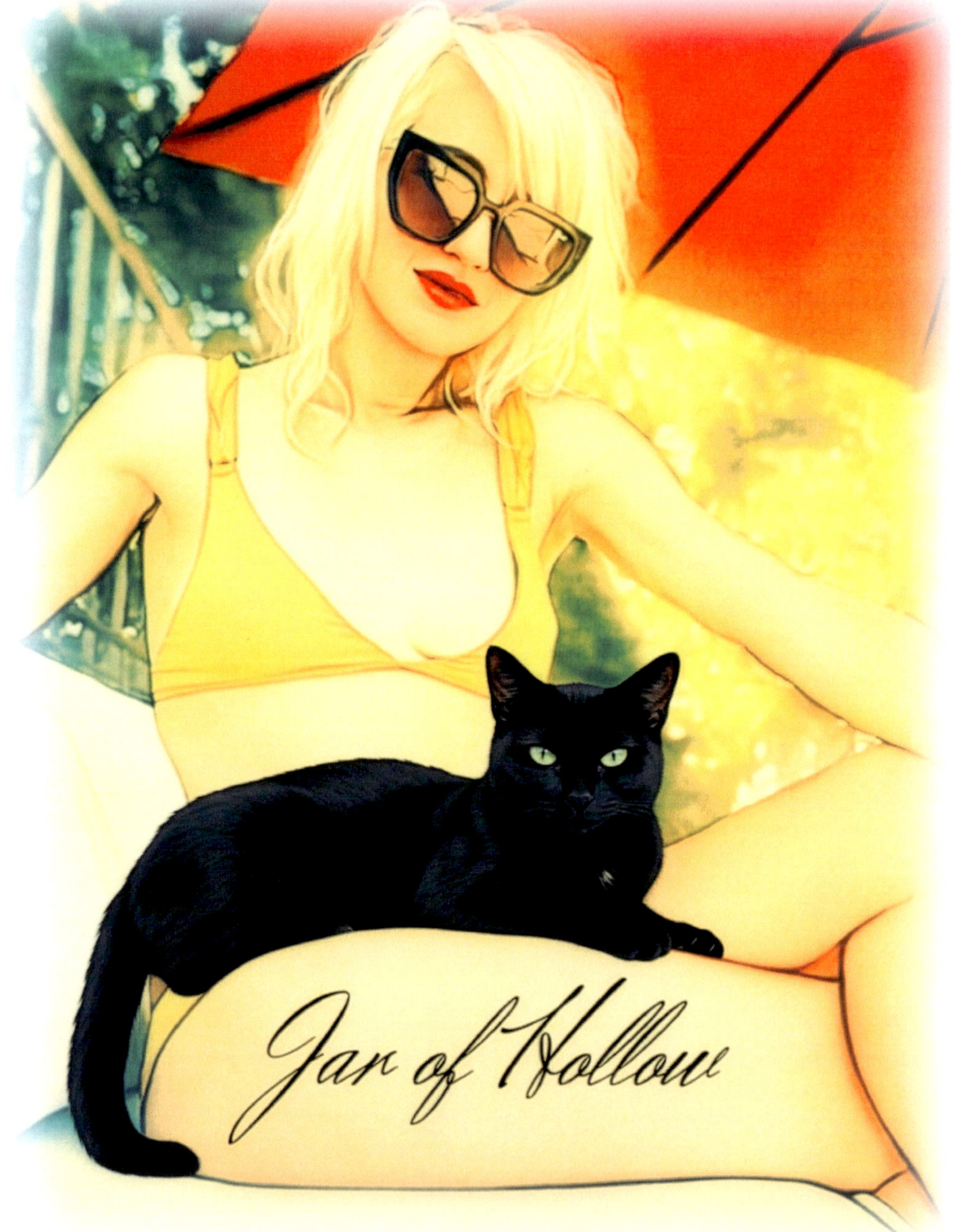
Jar of Hollow

Jar of Hollow

How emptiness can fill you.
Consumes all your space.
Your shadow is drawn,
Imbued with deep darkness.
Clutching a jar of hollow
With all that you have.
But if you gave it away,
Where would you be?

The enemy within.
I'm not willing to go with you
To where you're going to.
I'll stand here as where I am, and I'm not going to move.
I was meant to be here, exactly as I am.
Your darkness wasn't made for me.
I won't give you my hand.

You reached into the depths of me and raked me from within.
You threw me down a flight of stairs, with the carelessness of sin.
Broken, I am standing up and reclaiming my ground.
There's parts of me you can't get to, no matter where you're found.
Your strength is an illusion, you are destroyed by light.
You have no vow or purpose, but just a worthless might.

There's not a blow you'll spare me from,
A hurt that you won't cause.
There's nothing you won't take from me,
And you don't need applause.

As I lift myself from the ground, I turn my head to you.
I'll say it here and I'll say it once, and you'll know that it's true.
I'm not going with you, to the place you'd drag me to.
And now that I have made it clear, so comes the end of you.

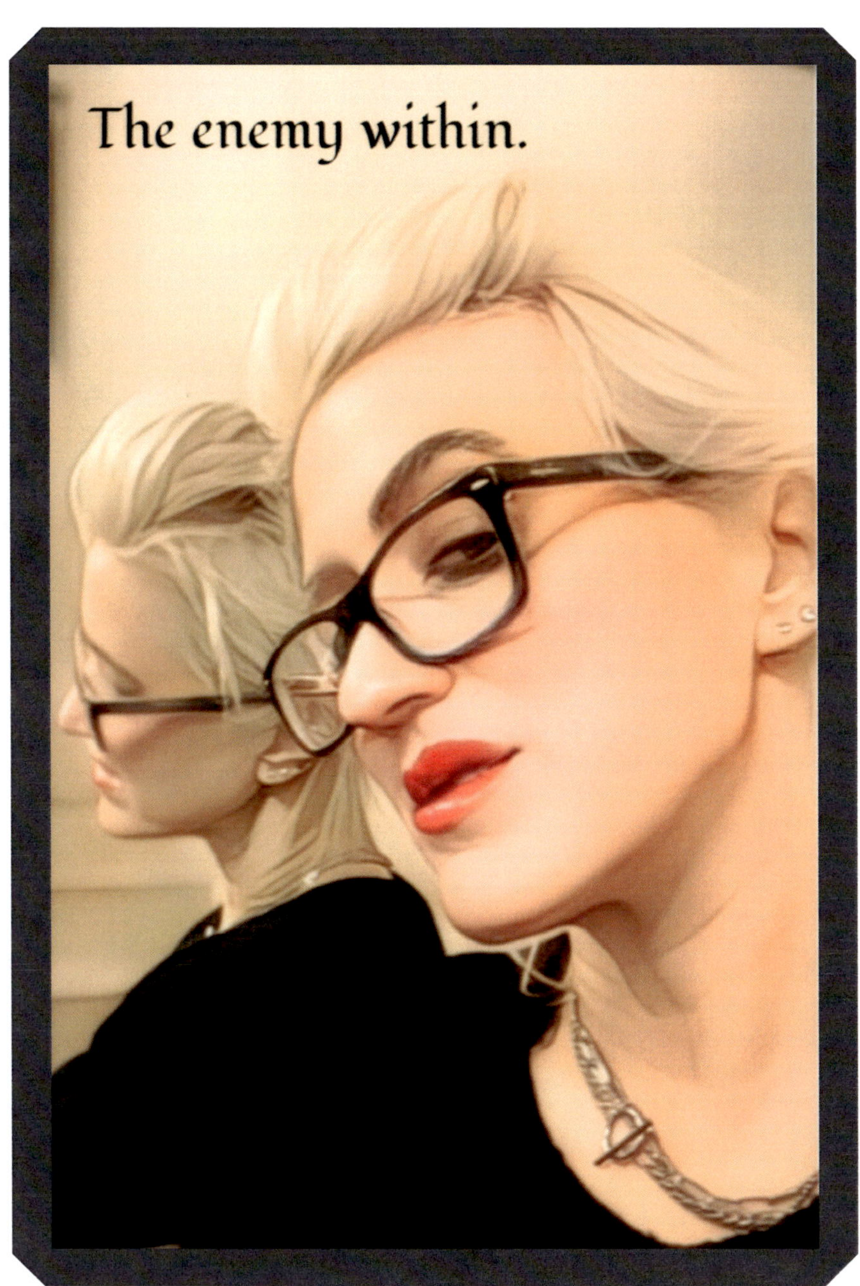
The enemy within.

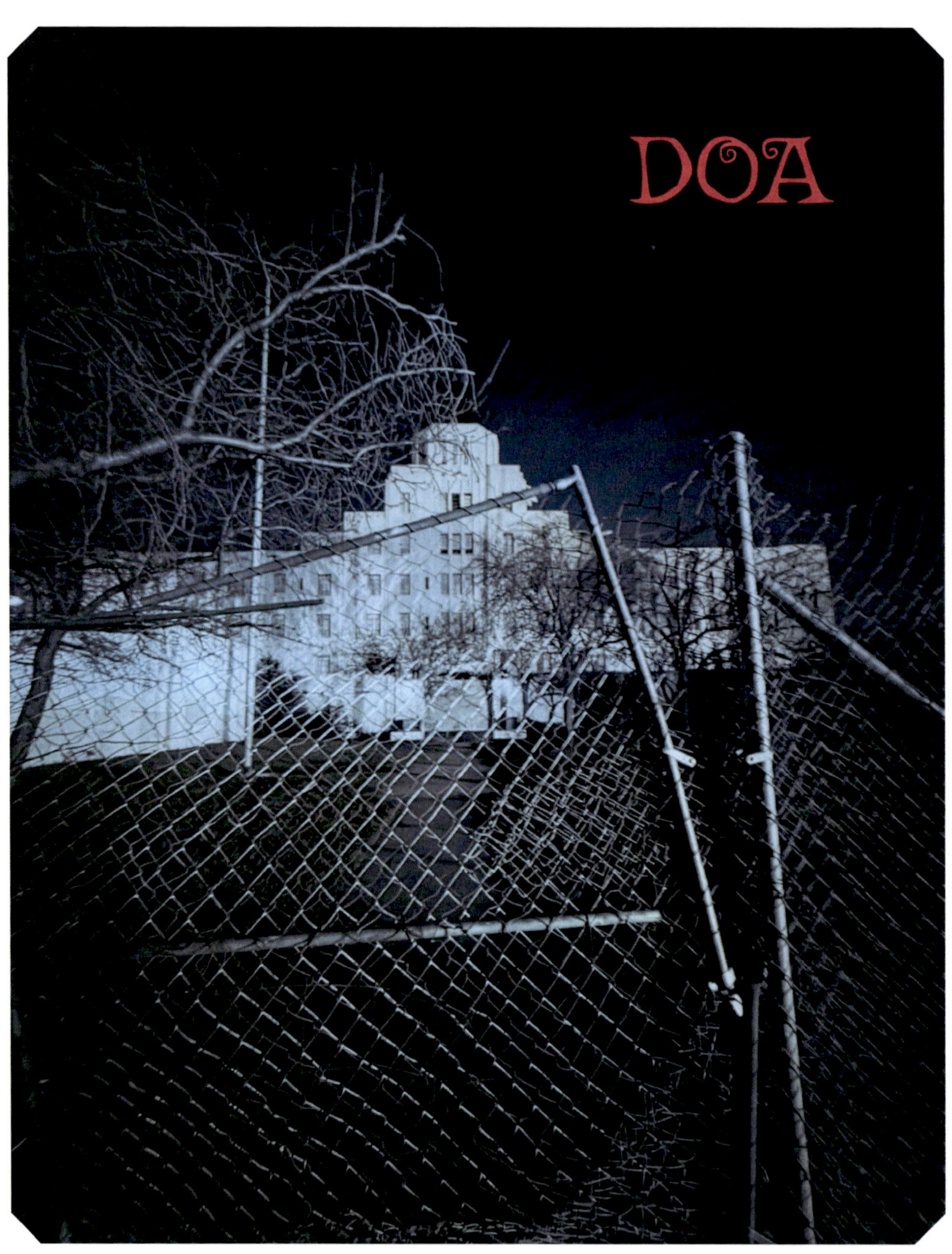
DOA

DOA.

You and me.
Time together seems will never be.
My heart with yours, deep to explore.
Yet in my time love's left ignored.

So move me,
I sit here and wait.
All paradise found beyond this gate.

Better yet, I'll go,
Now rushed with thrill.
This girl is me.
And move me?
Yeah, I will.

And then we were ashes.
Warm days joyful, endless in sight.
Photos of memories flashed and bright.
Began to tarnish, bubble and peel.
Clutching our dreams fading, so surreal.
Became fragile without care's salve in time.
The delicate exposed to the match's light.
Ignited and it all crashed down.
And then we were ashes.
Sadness unknown soon came to be.
Now I walk alone through embers, debris.
Where did you go, how were you lost?
Our union divine but with a cost.
How fleeting time would beat us still.
Lives outrunning cannot escape life's will.
No recourse found and cannot mend.
Caged in glass, sand drips to its end.
I close my eyes and see you there.
In all the light a wistful heart can spare.
I cannot erase and never will.
Our days in love, in my mind's eye still.
Fueled by darkness, set ablaze.
No safety for frail hearts mired in the maze.
Fleeing the reckless heartbreaking wrath,
Burned upon the fire's path.
And then we were ashes.

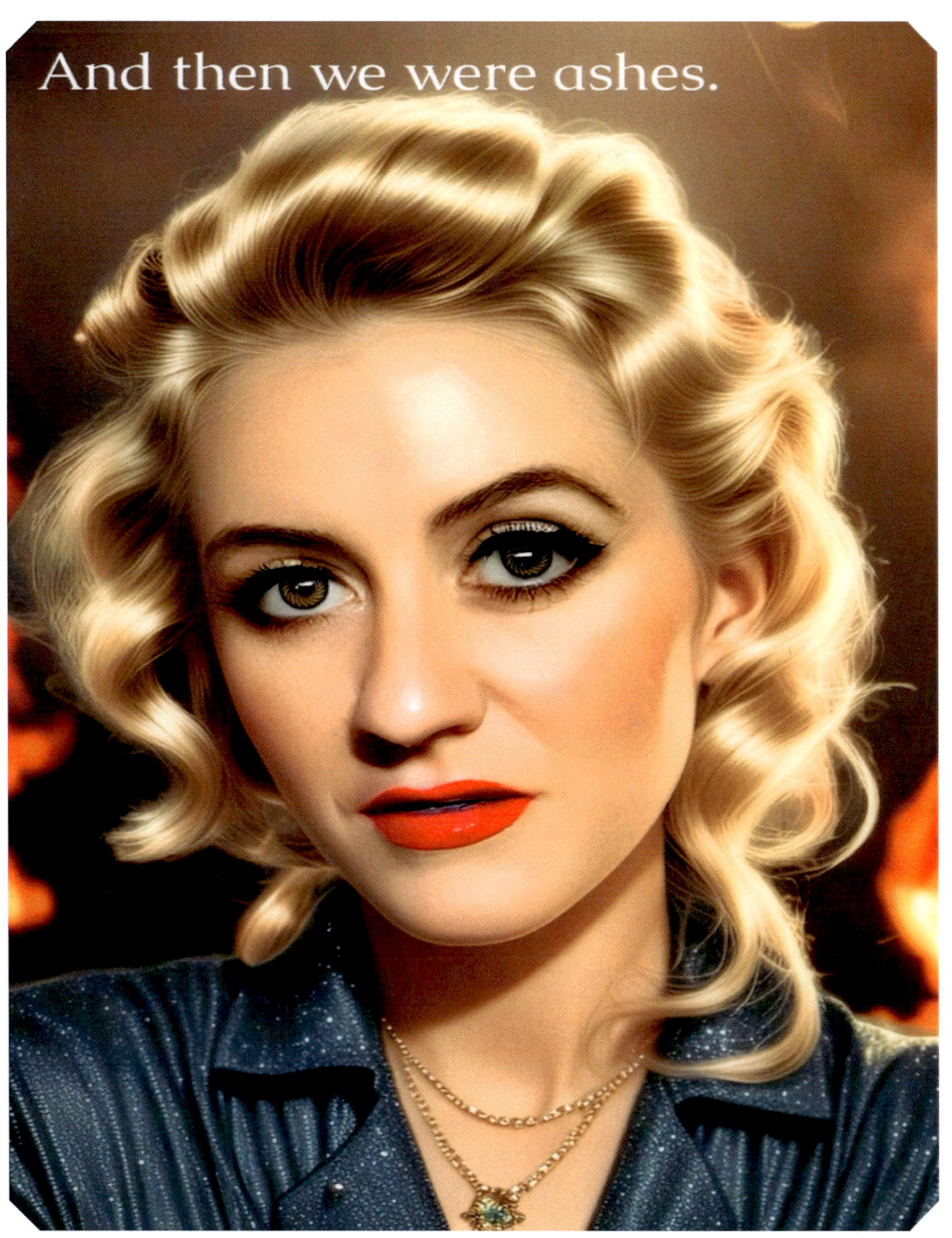
And then we were ashes.

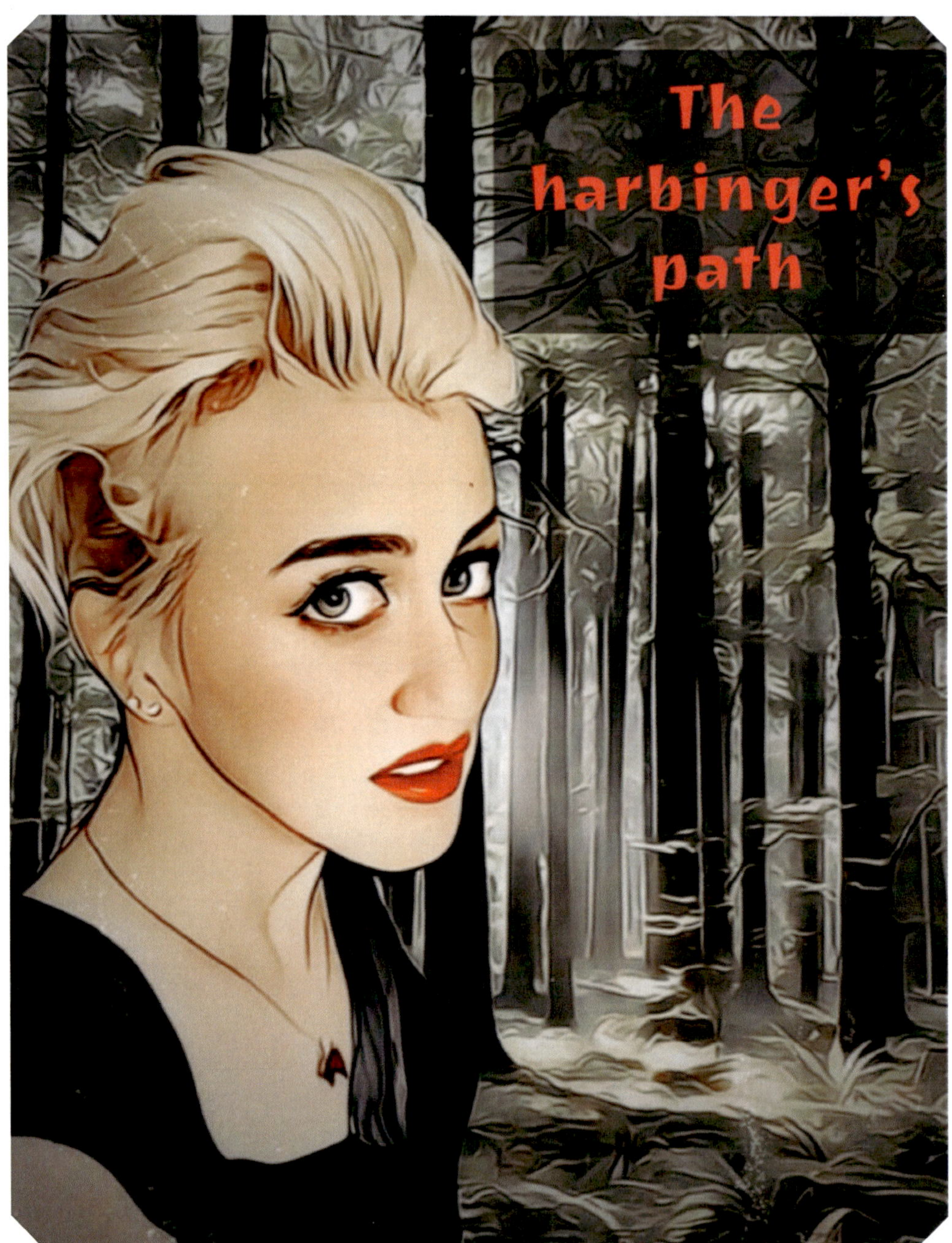
The
harbinger's
path

The harbinger's path (Original Version)

One day I was out for a walk,
The skies shining clear and bright.
A beautiful path lay before me, colors abound.
With an unexpected shift there was a cold chill.
The skies darkened for a moment,
As a cool breeze hid the sun behind quick moving clouds.
Upon this sudden dim, from the corners of brief darkness,
Figures emerged with shadows in their pockets.
Drawn with deep sullen eyes, they gathered around me,
And told me how my story ends.
To hear these words, I trembled.
How could it be?
Tears welled in my eyes, and in silence I wept.
A gentle breeze blew the clouds away.
They were gone, I had no answers.
I walked along but not the same.
As I listened to my breath with every step.
Graced by the sun's warmth, in the quiet still,
Along the gravel path.

The harbinger's path (Extended Version)

One day I was out for a walk,
Through a small clearing, in the serene and peaceful woods.
The skies were shining clear and bright,
Upon the beautiful path that lay before me, colors abound.
I carried along with the gentle sound of the breeze,
The tranquil echo of birds floating in the warm air.
Suddenly with an unexpected shift, there was a frigid chill.
The skies darkened, iced grey and shivering cold,
As a brisk wind hid the sun behind quick moving clouds.
Upon this sudden dim, from the corners of brief darkness,
Figures emerged with shadows in their pockets.
Effortlessly moving with grave purpose,
They slid from the forest's cast.
Drawn with deep sullen eyes, they gathered around me.
I froze, encircled, as I breathlessly scanned each ghostly presence.
Shrouding me in blackness,
Together they hummed a foreboding whisper,
And told me how my story ends.
To hear these words, I trembled.
How could it be?
Tears welled in my eyes, and in silence, I wept.
A gentle breeze blew the clouds away.
Just like that, the skies cleared, and they were gone.
I had no answers.
I walked along but not the same.
As I listened to my breath with every step,
Graced by the sun's warmth, in the quiet still.
Along the gravel path.

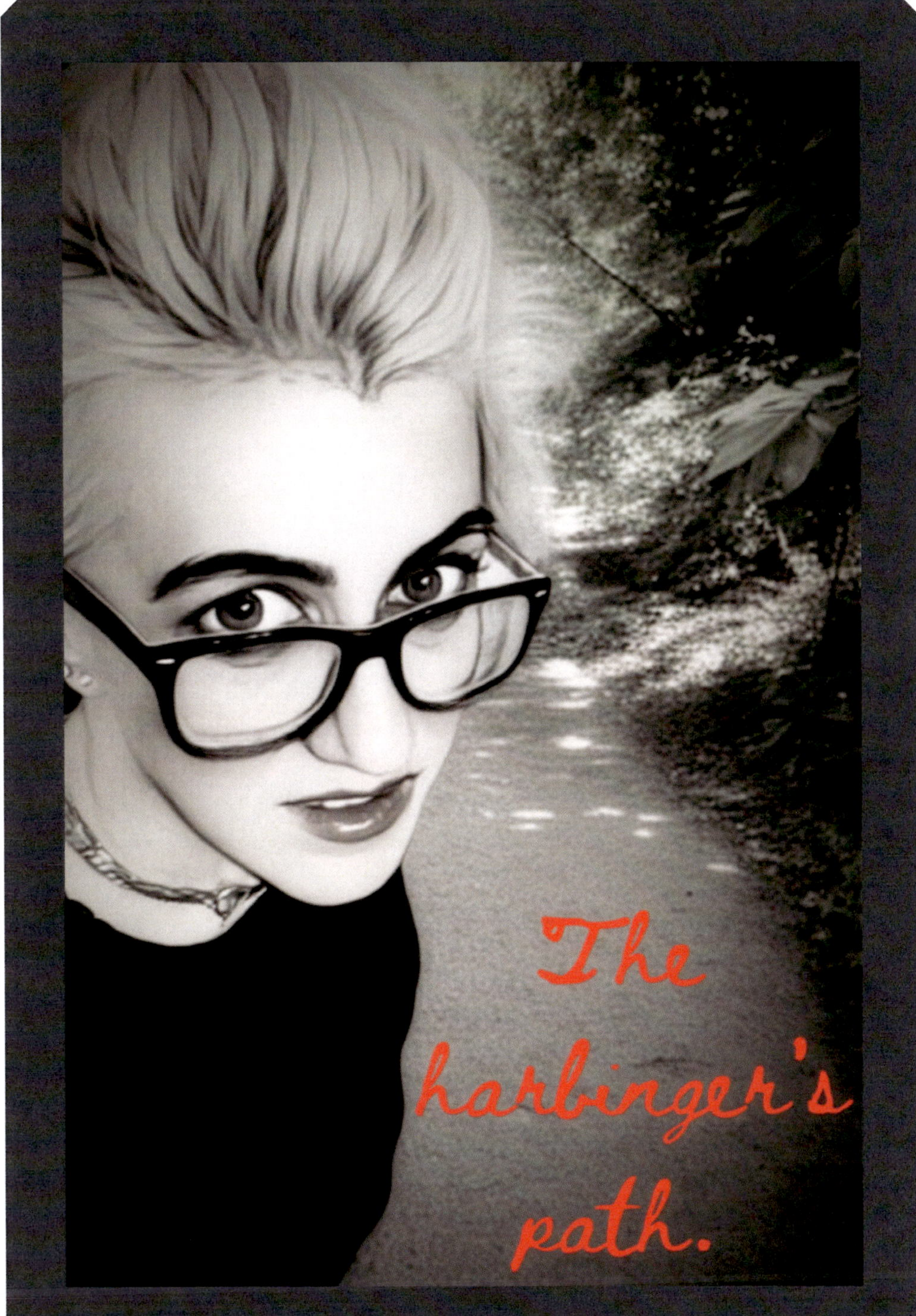
The
harbinger's
path.

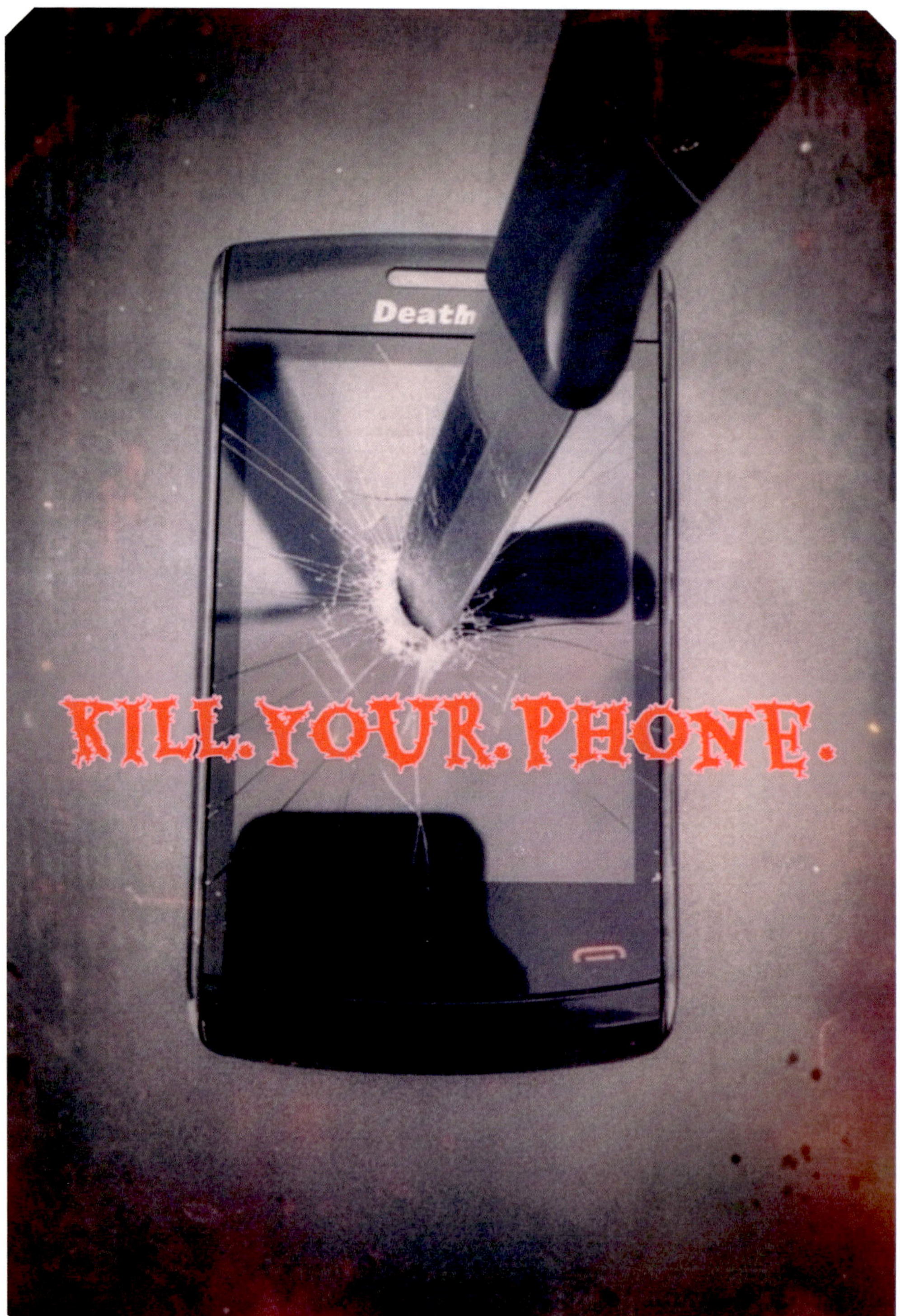
Death
KILL. YOUR. PHONE.

KILL.YOUR.PHONE.

Alive but mostly dead.
Will you spend your whole life being led?
Can't quite place the impending dread.
Kill your phone.
Since when was an image worth more than your life?
Anonymous lovers click your empty strife.
Hours of youth and you cannot move.
Nothing to show and will never prove.
Don't forget your humanity.
You're the one breathing, not the machine.
Kill.
Your.
Phone.
For me, I'm drawn to the blissful path.
Answers to life's questions, not the aftermath.
Everything this world stands to lose.
Connection, purpose, the touch that blooms.
Data driven outcomes are electronic trash.
The highest answer in your own mind's grasp.
Human above all, lest we forget.
The tools are our tools, we aren't their pets.
Enough of the nightmare, live real life.
A phone's a phone, it's not a knife.
Open your eyes and see the day.
Kill.
Your.
Phone.

The City of Hope.

I've come to you and prayed you were real.
Shining in the darkness, to save me from here.
The scars that I wear are now mine to keep.
Remembering my time before them, in quiet I weep.
Will I ever be the same or is there no return?
Innocence door now shut, for the sun-filled days I yearn.
I kneel on your doorstep, my arms outstretched.
Now weaker than I could have ever guessed.
As I bow my head, I whisper my only ask,
Will you take me by my hands?
Will you be my City of Hope?
Healing then came within my darkest depths.
Pain through pain with every moment and breath.
Glimpses of chance, at times knocked down.
Climbing back on my feet, facing fears profound.
Recovery with no certain path, the arc of time unknown.
Now I am forever changed, a secret blessing shown.
My own strength revealed in uncertain tides.
Knowing with every crest, life's brief thrilling ride.
I would never have been here to have these days.
In strange time now I know, none of us are saved.
Where would I be, myself alive?
The vision of a horizon where once again I can thrive.
Thank you for every day that you fight.
To be our beacon, to be our light.
To be our chance, to be our dreams.
To be our City of Hope.

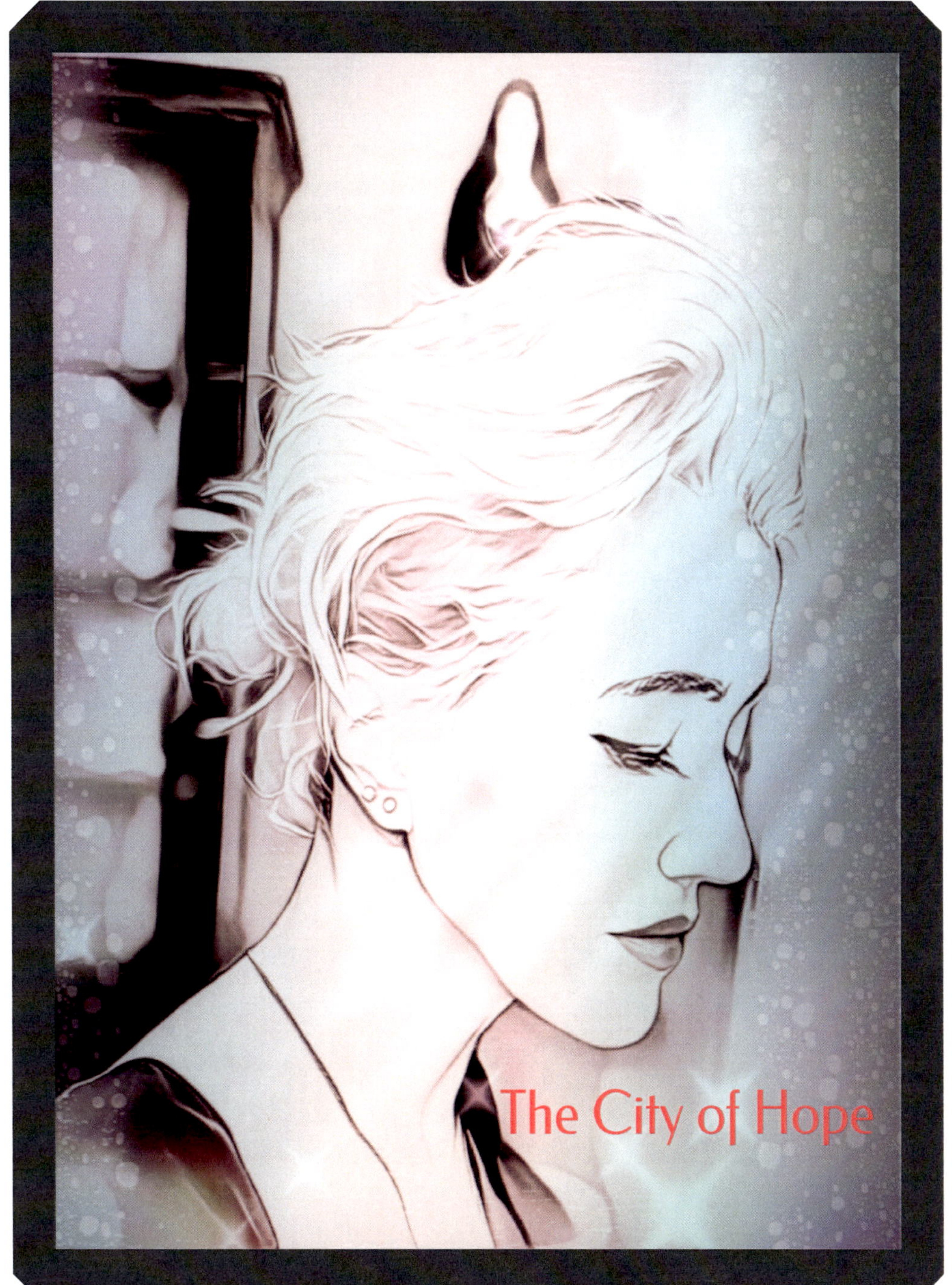
The City of Hope

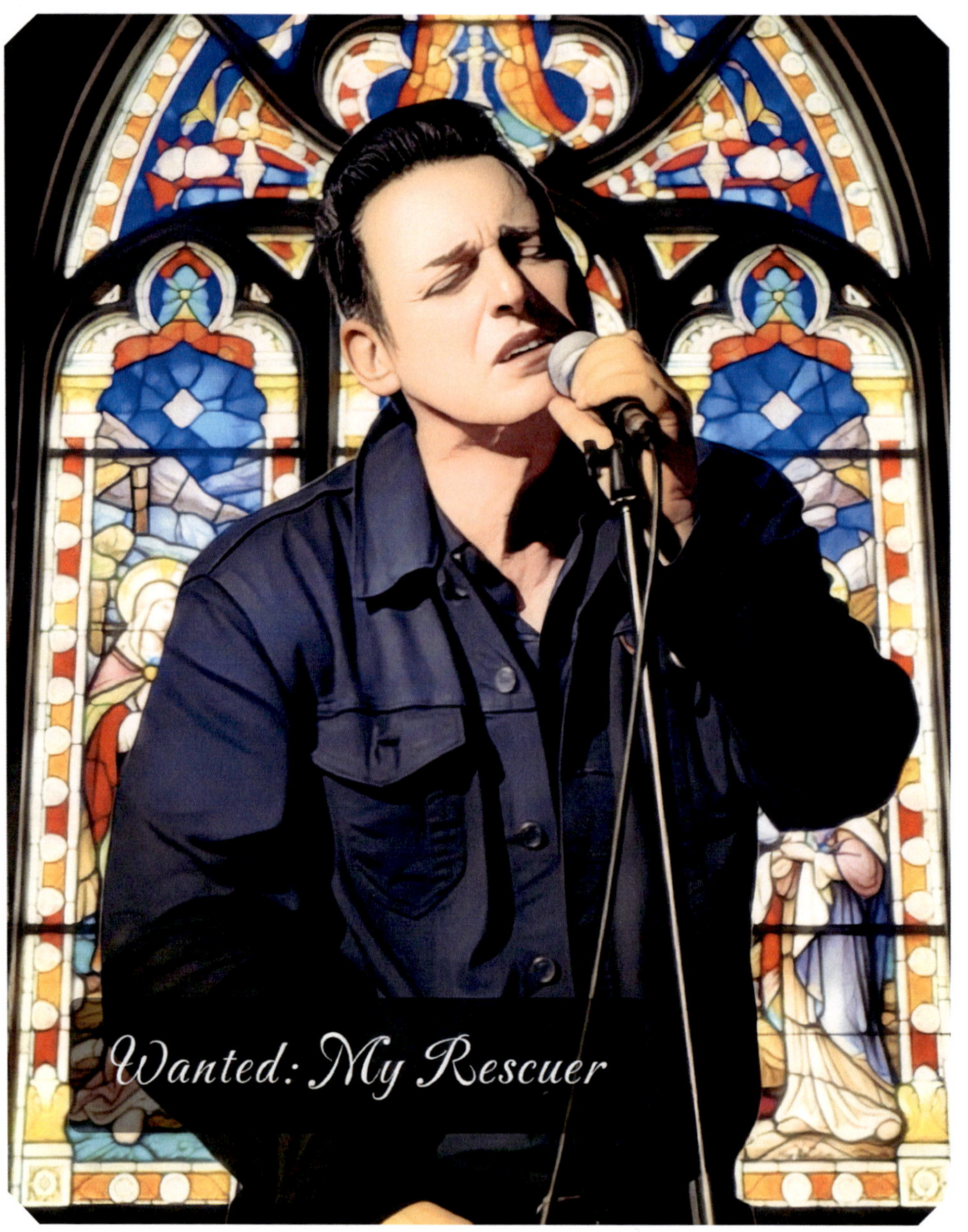
Wanted: My Rescuer

Wanted: My rescuer

All I ever wanted was to be rescued.
I must have read too many fairytales.
My one true love would come and save me.
Up into the clouds, we'd forever sail.
I cannot believe that I met you,
So much time had passed.
I thought I was having young girl fantasies,
Until you showed me a love that lasts.
We have endless days in the sunshine,
Times I dream should never pass.
But real life comes and finds me,
And takes me down so fast.
A woman must be in her place,
Or how the world will let her know.
All around her will come crashing down,
When she isn't where she's supposed to go.
Now I sit here among the ordinary.
The technicolor has gone out again.
How I miss your smile so deeply,
Without a message or a picture I could send.
I'll do my best to be like the others,
Do my job, pay my bills and go out.
Until again I can have you,
My heart is left apart.

My Narcissist Fantasy

The submissive provider is what you seek.
With profound strength and the appearance of weak.
Should I slay the work but not take the credit?
Share my ideas but claim you said it.
Make the money and say it's yours.
Time with you is such a chore.
Can't say thanks and nothing nice.
That's when I now will draw the knife.
To cut the cord and set you free.
To drown someone else in your endless needs.
The perfect one is out there for you.
Who enjoys the feel of their face on your shoe.
Me, I'm gone I think it's best.
You've convinced me I'm not quite up to test.
I'd say I'll miss you but it's not true.
That idea is yours, and I'll give the credit to you.

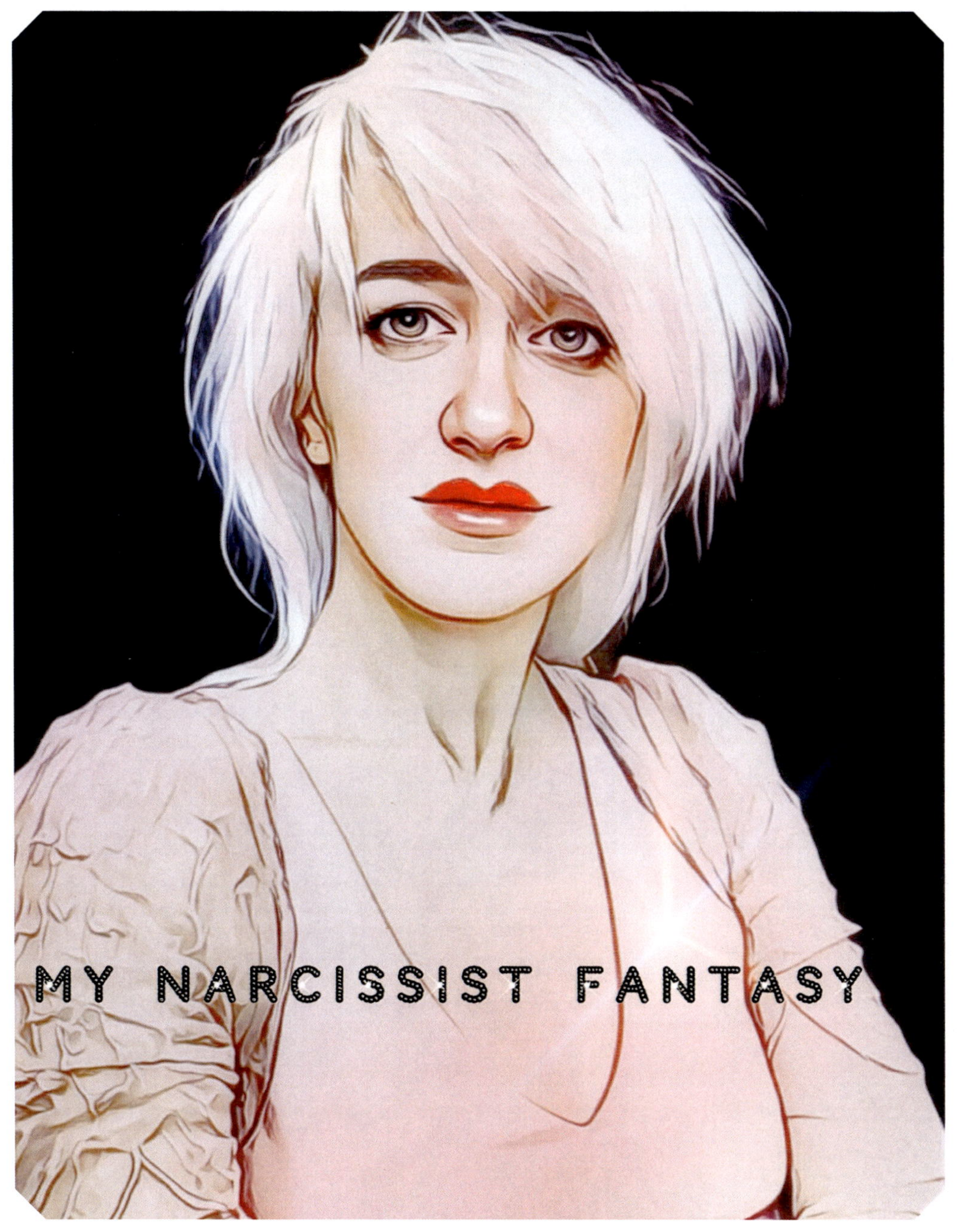
MY NARCISSIST FANTASY

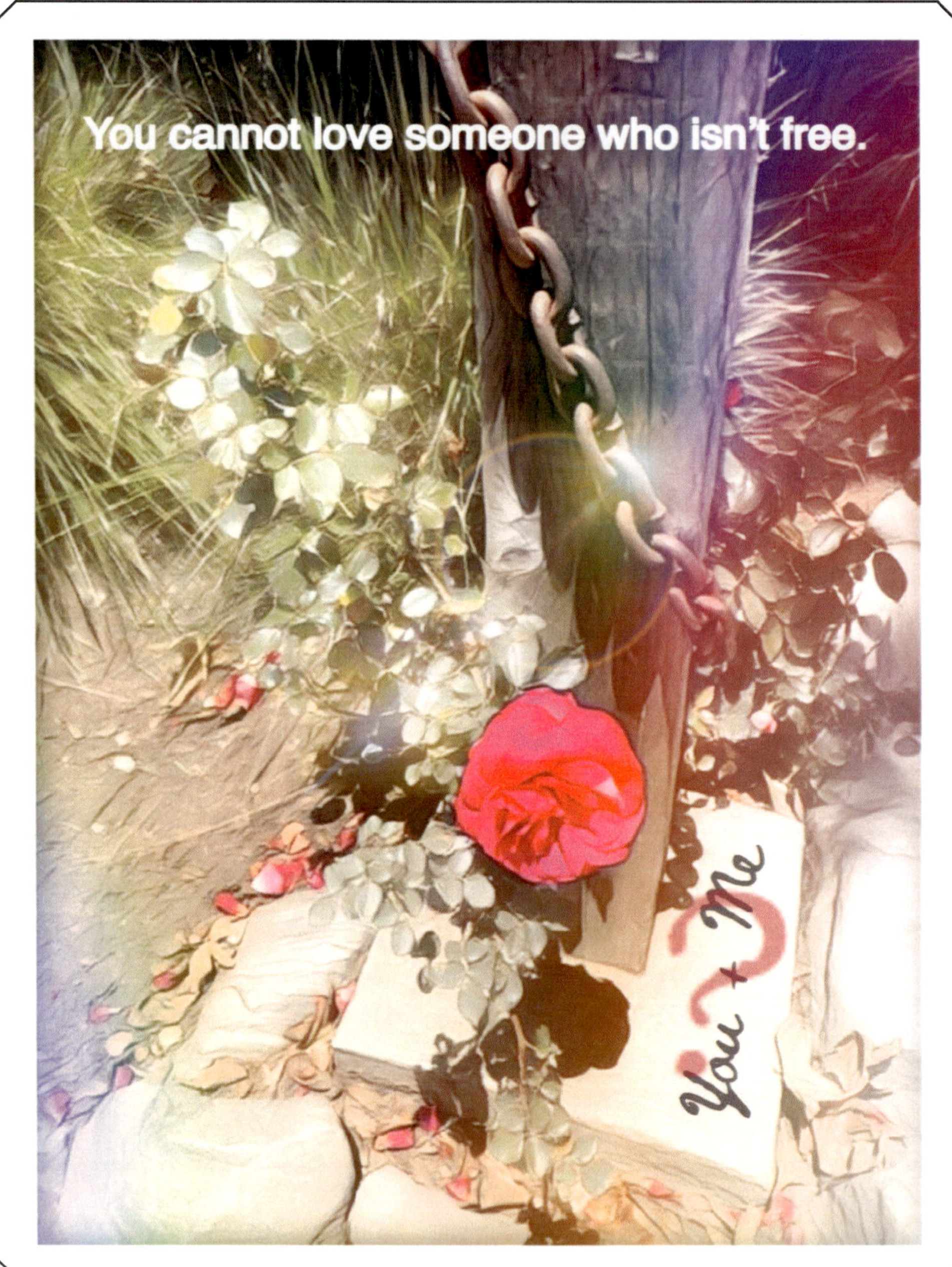
You cannot love someone who isn't free.
You + Me

You cannot love someone who isn't free.
Was never yours,
And will not be.

I'll never love anyone how I love you.
I'm old enough to know that's true.
In our prisons alone we weep.
I can't free you,
And you can't free me.

Yet the key rests hidden inside your hand.
And I'll wait for you forever,
As only my heart can stand.

The end of the beginning.
And not the beginning of the end.
Today reveals a new day,
As I rise and pray to mend.
Uncertainty has thrust me into restless, heaving tides.
Awash unto abandoned shores,
I gasp with tearing eyes.
Covered with the scars inside of battles I have fought.
Tattered, worn, and bruised, I cried.
Pain I could not wrest till naught.

May it be I have another chance to breathe as me again?
To heal the wounds I carry forth,
Time will tell if not to bend.
Blue skies now clear yet wary of the clouds that lurk afar.
Will they drive the rains that wash me down,
And flood hope's door ajar.

I wipe the grit and dust the sands that graze my weighted brow.
For I do not know how far I'll tread,
Pace each step with life avowed.
To will the end of the beginning,
Facing the beginning of the end.
And with this gift of newfound strength,
Breakthrough my path's portend.

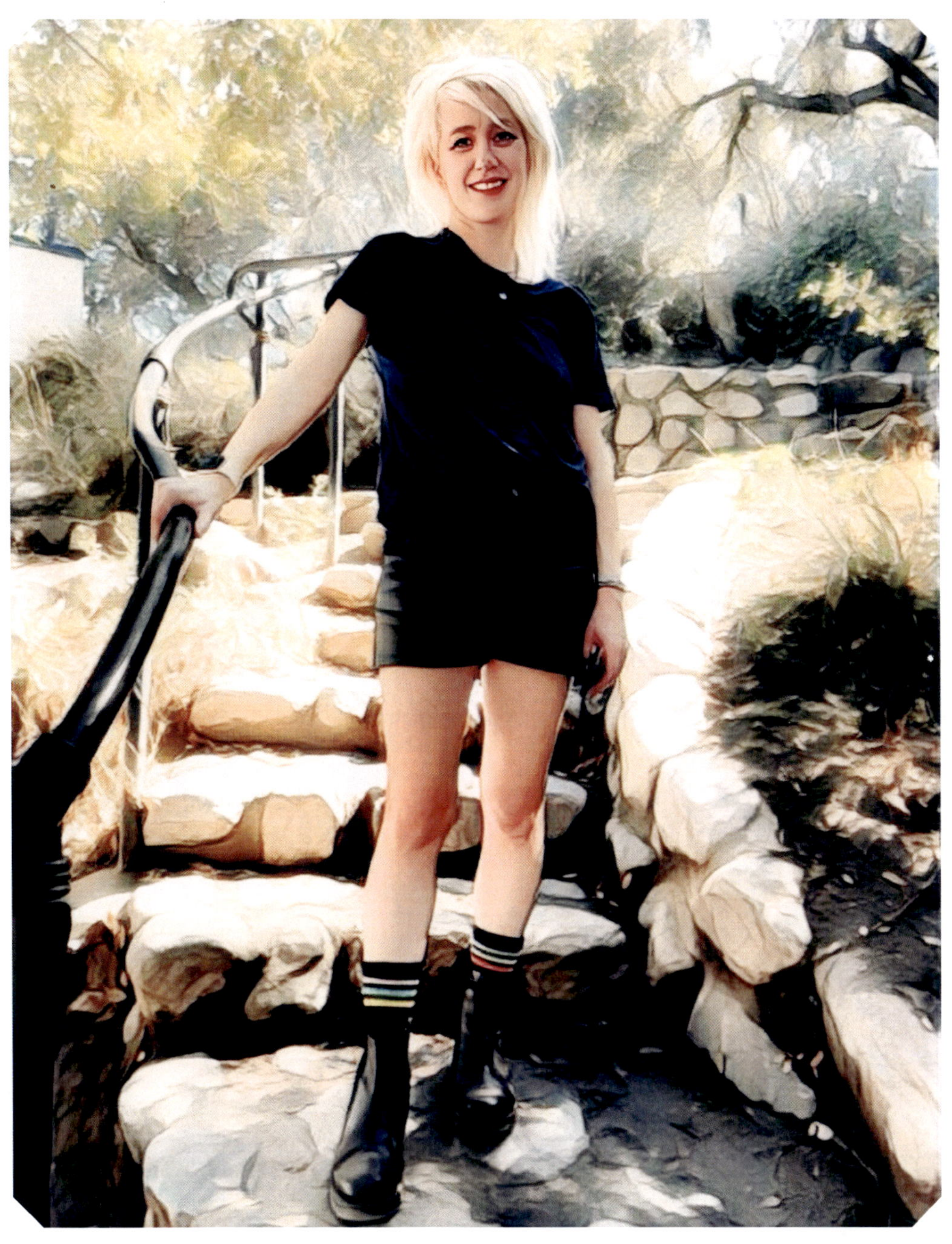

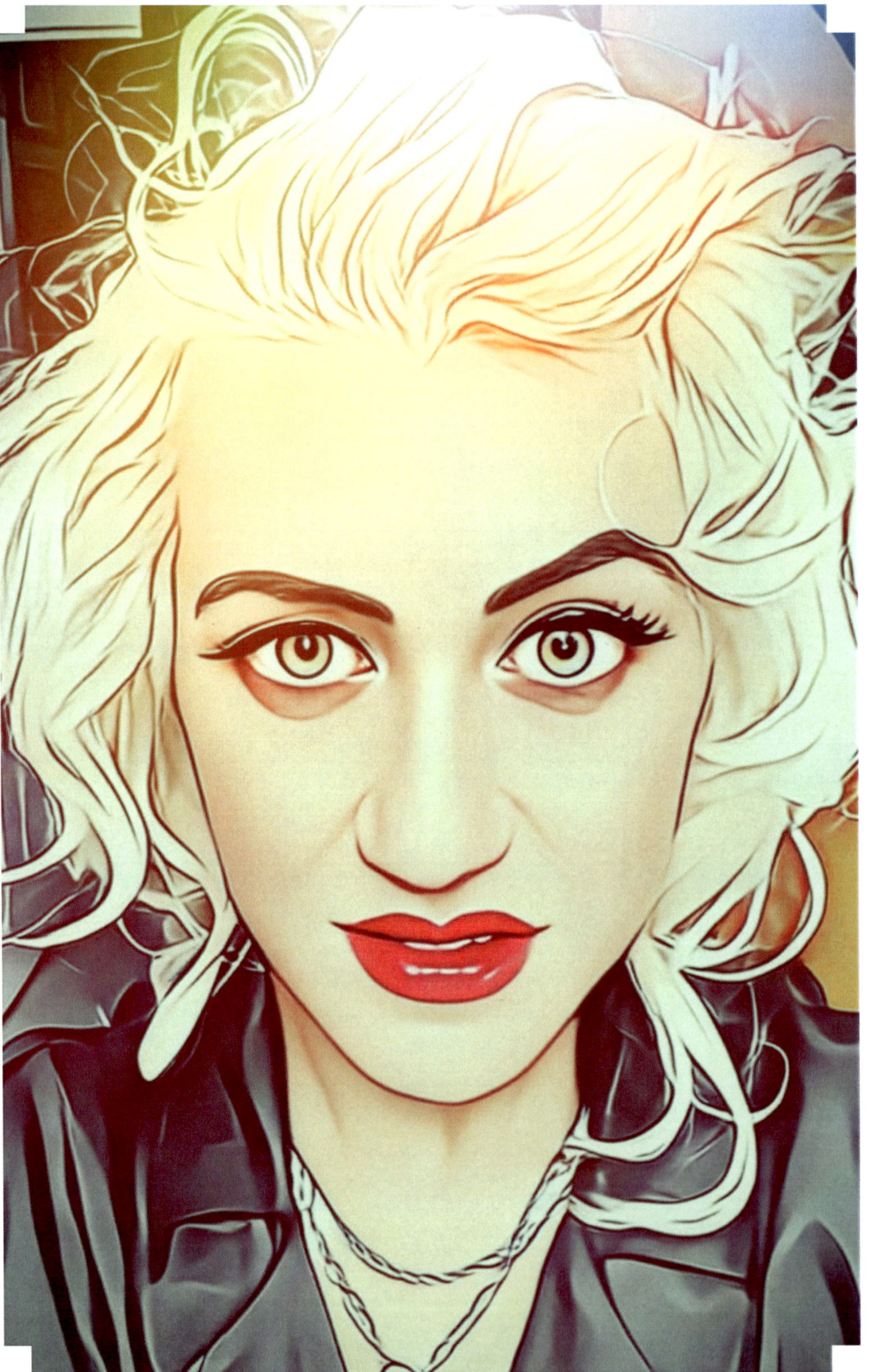

A HEART FULL OF LOVE HAS MORE STRENGTH THAN THE WORLD CAN BEAR...

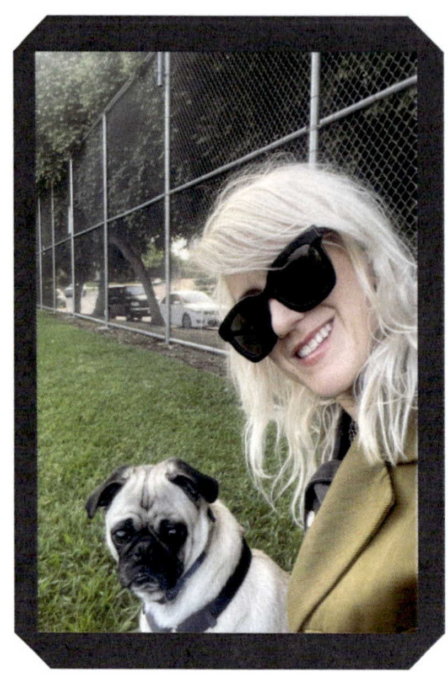

Emmet the Pug & the author

ACKNOWLEDGEMENTS

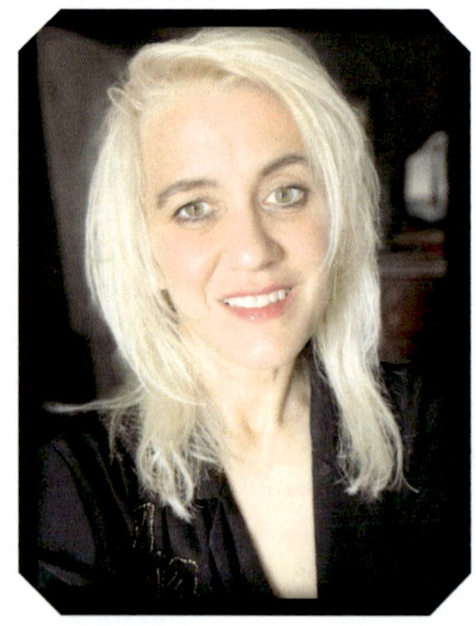

Sue Chaplin, the author

ABOUT THE AUTHOR

Sue Chaplin was born and raised in Vernon, Connecticut. She attended the University of Connecticut for her undergraduate studies. After living briefly in Boston, Massachusetts, she has lived and worked in Los Angeles, California since 2002. She is grateful to call Pasadena home, which she shares with her love, Alain, sons, Peter and Gavin, and pug, Emmet. A lover of creativity, invention, and imagination, she enjoys exploring possibility and richness in life through writing, innovation and artistic expression.

A mind's piece is a powerful, intimate journey through the depths of the human heart, where darkness and beauty live side by side. Written across years marked by transformation, loss, rebirth, love, fantasy, and fierce resilience, this stunning collection opens a window into the raw, unfiltered experience of being fully alive.

Sue Chaplin's voice is fearless. Her poems move from quiet heartbreak to blazing hope, from surreal dreams to the stark truth of self-discovery. Each piece unfolds as a snapshot of emotion, captured in vivid language and paired with evocative visual artistry that bridges reality and imagination.

Inside this book, you'll find:

- Poems born from love, loss, and rediscovery.
- Meditations on identity, freedom, longing, and truth.
- A visual tapestry blending photography with creative expression.
- A heartfelt sharing the author's inspiring personal journey.
- A collection arranged in the order written, letting you travel the emotional arc as it unfolded in real time.

A mind's piece is for readers who:

- Seek writing that feels real: emotional, brave, and human.
- Find meaning in life's extremes: despair and joy, solitude-and connection.
- Love work that blends visual art with literary expression.
- Believe in the power of poetry to heal, reveal, and reimagine life and oneself.

Step inside and find your own piece of mind.

www.ingramcontent.com/pod-product-compliance
Lightning Source LLC
LaVergne TN
LVRC090253110826
845147LV00007B/732